60 minutes with...
A David Knight Company
THE LIMITED EDITION SIGNED AUDIO CD

The Chelsea experience

From those that should know...

Harris-Dixon-Bonetti-Tambling

With David Knight

This edition January 2009

Copyright 2008 The Executive Solution

No part of this book may be transmitted or reproduced in any form or by any means without written permission from The Executive Solution, except by a reviewer who wishes to quote brief passages in connection with a review

ISBN 978-1-4092-5294-8

Visit www.60mins.tv for signed copies and live tour information

With special thanks to Mark Conlon for putting hours of audio interview into text format

Mark Conlon is a freelance football writer, and has worked with legends of the game, such as George Cohen, Peter Bonetti, Ron Harris, Bobby Tambling and Kerry Dixon.

With a degree in Sports Journalism, he has written for *60mins.tv* and *Front*, and his work can be also be accessed on-line, at both *cfcnet.co.uk* and *overtimeonline.co.uk*. and via Hayters Sports Agency

David J Knight is best known for being the creator of the 60 minutes with... series. David has worked alongside 40 plus legends in 2008 and continues to be a popular figure within the world of football.

This book is dedicated to all the fans that support their teams week in, week out!

KERRY DIXON

The real-life Roy of the Rovers. Prolific, and popular with the fans

How does it feel to be spoken about as a football legend?

I'm very honored ….it depends how people see the word legend. I think for years service, what you actually achieve, Some people will be called legend for whatever reason, and like a lot of other things, like 'world class', it sometimes gets used far too easily, but if people want to call me that I'm more than happy, and very proud to be associated with that name.

Who or what, inspired you to become a footballer?

I suppose my dad really. He was really the one. He was a footballer himself, we watched football, he used to take me to football when I was a kid. I loved playing the game myself. There certainly wasn't an inspiration in terms of a player, I used to go and watch Luton Town as a kid, stood on the terraces, played for them as a boy in their youth sides, or academy sides as they're called now, but sadly for me, at the age of 16 they booted me out. However, not to be deterred, the rest is history as they say.

When as a young kid, you get told that you're not going to make it as a footballer, how do you take that? Did you think that your chance had gone or did you feel as determined as ever with a belief that you were going to make it?

I always believed that I could make it, and I also believed that there was a lot of luck involved. I got told that I wasn't going to make it twice. The first time by David Pleat, who was youth team manager at Luton at the time. He decided that he wasn't going to take me on as an apprentice, that was at the age of 16. I think they took 13 apprentices that year, some good players, but he decided he wasn't going to take me, and they let me go, which was a bit devastating really.

Nonetheless, I had to go and do something, so I went and got a tool-making job, got an apprenticeship, and I spent five years at College actually getting my indentures. Having said that, I hated every minute of it, I didn't like being in a factory at all, and I haven't been back in one since the day I left.

You said you'd been released twice. Who was the other club you got released by Kerry?

Well, how it worked was, at the age of 16 I got released by Luton and did an apprenticeship. But I was also playing football, and I went non-league with a fella called Brendan McNalliot, to Chesham Utd. He's a friend of my dad's, and he played for Luton. He played in the 1959 Cup Final, he played with my dad, who played for Luton and Coventry, and he gave me a chance. I played in the reserves, got in the first team as a 16 year old, and scored goals.

Spurs saw me playing, they came and gave me a trial and liked what they saw. Peter Shreeves, who was the reserve team manager at the time, decided to offer me an apprenticeship at Spurs, but I had to decline because I was already doing an apprenticeship tool-making. I wasn't going to give that up, because with an apprenticeship you could be told no again, and then you've lost your trade, so I decided to keep my trade, and Spurs took me on as a part-time pro.

They gave me a part-time pro contract for a year, and I finished top-scorer in the youth team, 32 goals in the South East Counties it was, but sadly at the end of the season, I was told that they weren't going to offer me a deal, because I was too old for the youth team, and at the time, they had people like Mark Falco, Terry Gibson, Colin Lee, and Ian Moores, all playing up-front, and who would have all been ahead of me, even in the reserves, so they decided to let me go, and that was a gutter as well.

So then I went non-league, went back with Brendan McNalliot, and moved on to Dunstable, which was my local club, and I loved every minute of it. Reading finally saw me when I scored 52 goals, which was a Southern League record at the time, and Maurice Evans signed me for Reading.

Can you pinpoint when you heard of Reading's interest in you?

Well, clubs were being linked with me all the time, and there was always rumours scouts would be watching. I just loved playing for Dunstable. When I got released by Spurs, I had offers from Orient, Brentford, and some other London clubs to go for trials, but I wasn't interested. It worked for me once at Dunstable, and I believed in my own ability.

I'd have been in the third year of my apprenticeship now as a tool-maker, I hated it, but I was determined to finish. I have an inner determination when I want to do things, and I was determined to finish that, so I played non-league, and Reading was the club that came in for me with a £20,000 bid.

What were your first impressions of Reading as a club?

I loved the idea of being a full-time footballer, but having said that, the first year I was combining as a part-time pro once again, to finish my apprenticeship. I got Friday's off at the factory so I could train with the team and prepare for Saturday's game, and I had to work extra hours during the week, so I had four long days, and one day off.

I trained Friday with the team, played on a Saturday, and I had to go up and train on either a Tuesday or Wednesday depending. I've got to say, the people where I was doing my apprenticeship were very accommodating in allowing me to be a pro.

What do you remember about your first team debut for Reading?

At Brentford, I think I scored in a 2-1 win, a tap-in from a yard. It wasn't a trademark, but anyone who knows me, knows my goals come from everywhere, and I don't care how they go in, as long as my name's on the scoresheet.

Were you one of these players who used to practice goal celebrations on the training pitch, doing triple back-flips and that sort of thing?

No, I think that's a sign of the times that came when the TV exposure increased. I did a few where my arms were aloft; it was just what you felt at the time. Sometimes I'd jump up, I never did any rolling over, or running around flags or any of that. I used to run, hug team-mates, arms aloft, that sort of thing, so no, it was a much more traditional approach I'm afraid, boring some might say.

How would you describe the feeling of scoring a goal, to somebody who has never played the game before?

It's the greatest feeling anyone could ever have. Of course there are things in life that would cause more emotion, but scoring a goal......I mean it wasn't the greatest goal I scored, but I scored at the clock end at Highbury when I made my First Division debut. There must have been I don't know how many thousands of Chelsea fans in there, but when I volleyed in a goal past the great Pat Jennings, and an international back-four, it was an amazing scene and an amazing experience. To score a goal in the First Division was something I'll never forget.

You scored an amazing 51 goals in 116 appearances for Reading. What goals stand out?

I don't know where they got the extra six appearances, I thought it was 110; I was always good on my stats. Which goal stands out? I don't know, but I remember playing against Watford in a full-members cup tie I think it was, one of the lower trophies we played for in those days, it may have been the old League Cup I'm not sure.

We beat them 5-1 and I scored a goal in that, but during the course of my final year at Reading, I was being linked with so many clubs, and ultimately it was Chelsea who signed me, but Watford, and Graham Taylor tells the story now that he would have signed me, but he watched me too many times and couldn't make up his mind, because I had a good game, poor game, average game, good game, and he said he learnt something from me. He said go and watch a player, if you like something, sign them, and he's kept to that ever since.

How do you look back at your time at Reading now?

I loved my time at Reading. The first year was as a part-time pro, and the second year wasn't as productive. I was full-time, and thought I'd improve, but the improvement didn't come immediately. It was really in my final year that I set it alight, and I became top-scorer in the old Third Division, and that was the thing that got clubs interested in me and set me on my way.

I'll never forget Maurice Evans for giving me the chance. Sadly he passed away, great man, and he gave me the opportunity, he had faith in me. He signed players such as John Aldridge, Neil Webb, and Lawrie Sanchez. That Reading side was a good side.

How aware were you that the Chelsea deal almost collapsed. They were haggling over a £25,000 fee because you were going to go and play for England?

Roger Smea was the Chairman, and Ken Bates at Chelsea, so if you knew those two, you'd know why they'd haggle over £25,000. At the time I wasn't really aware of it all. The papers were speculating, but it happened. Chelsea really came out of the blue, it only came to light afterwards that they were haggling.

Ken Bates just turned up one day in his Rolls-Royce, and Roger Smea said: "You're not going training, you're going to Aberystwyth to train with Chelsea, the Chairman will be here soon, so if you need some stuff, get it together", and that was it. Batesey had already talked me into joining Chelsea on that trip, but I didn't let him know because we still hadn't decided the wages, but I was convinced I wanted to join Chelsea.

What were your first impressions of Chelsea?

I hated the Aberystwyth training camp. If I wasn't convinced, and I already was, that first day running on the sand dunes was really hard. John Neal was the manager; I met him, Ian McNeil and John Hollins down there. McNeill was the assistant, and Hollins was the coach. I hated pre-season anyway, the physical side, and they told me if I wanted to sign, I had to go back the next day.

If you weren't a fan of pre-season training, what sort of trainer were you?

A lazy trainer really. I didn't do any more or any less than others. I loved shooting practice, I loved 5 a-sides, and I loved sprints on a Friday. I liked all the things I was good at, and hated the things I wasn't, like long-distance running and that sort of thing.

Any funny stories from the training ground spring to mind?

Numerous fights, there were fights all the time, and David Speedie was in most of them. Some of the funnier times came with Speedie under the Hollins regime. That was probably the greatest side I played in, with Pat Nevin and Speedie. That first year at Chelsea, we won the Second Division. We had some great characters, and I finished top-scorer, so I'd been top-scorer in the Third Division with Reading, and then the Second Division with Chelsea.

That was a fairytale season, arguably the greatest season of my life. I went on to finish top-scorer in the First Division, so it was 3, 2, and 1, in consecutive years. The season in the Second, we weren't fancied at all. Chelsea almost went down the season before; they only stayed up after a win at Bolton thanks to a Clive Walker goal. Six new faces were bought in by Ken Bates, and I was one of them.

We opened the season 25-1 for promotion, at home to Derby, who were favourites for the title under Peter Taylor, and we trounced them 5-0. I scored a couple, and from then on it was a fairytale. Chelsea fans who you speak to, who went to these games, they went to Brighton soon after, where we won 2-1, and they invaded the pitch and broke the crossbar, but it was out of exuberance, they couldn't believe the start we'd had. I scored both at Brighton, and I think to this day, it's why fans take you to their hearts, because you shared your experiences with them.

Do you think that's maybe missing in the game nowadays?

Yes, I look at Chelsea, and I think it's missing. The modern players don't get close enough to the fans. I think more players should spend time with the fans. People like Joe Cole, John Terry, and Frank Lampard are absolutely fantastic in having time for the fans, that's why those players will go down as legends in Chelsea fans hearts, because they say: "Hold on; I'm privileged, and these people have waited for my autograph", and instead of having a phone to their ear, they actually have time for fans. Those three are good examples of modern day players, but a lot of it is missing these days.

When we talk about the modern game, the profile of football has gone through the roof in terms of media coverage. How do you think you would have coped in today's game, having paparazzi outside your house waiting for an exclusive, and looking through your bins for wage slips?

To be fair, it did happen to a degree. Newspapers were equally as scathing towards players as they are today, it's just that the exposure today is a lot more, and it's really a case of players lives are in the spotlight. People say they get paid accordingly, and fair do's, but it's not easy.

I remember Gazza, who was probably the biggest star, used to have four newspaper men camped at the end of his drive all the time. Apparently one of the guys asked him to sign a football. When he gave Gazza the ball, he just booted it into the river and told them to clear off. They want to write stories about him, but they still want his signature, that's the hypocrisy of it all.

How good was Pat Nevin, for a striker like you?

He was an amazing player. Chelsea fans said he reminded them of Charlie Cooke previously. He was a dribbler, a wing-wizard. I found it hard at first to understand the way he would play, but our understanding developed. He would continually beat players. In a game against Newcastle, he beat about five players, and he even beat one player twice, the Chelsea fans were cheering, it was amazing.

You also spoke about David Speedie. It's been rumoured that you didn't get on off the pitch, is that true?

No. At first David was big mates with Colin Lee, and the three of us were vying for place in the side. Me and Colin started the first six games, and David didn't get in the side. When he did get in the side, he thought Colin should be playing as well. It culminated in a game against Man-City. He didn't pass to me, and we had a row, it continued up the tunnel, and in the dressing-room, we exchanged blows.

It got stopped, and John Neal called us in the office. He told us he thought we were both great strikers and we were his first choice two, so that was that. Colin Lee ended the season playing at right-back.

When it did click for you and Speedie, it really clicked. You were able to read each others game really well. What was the secret behind that?

He did the things that I didn't do so well, and vice-versa. It became so compatible, it was almost telepathic between us, and it gave us that extra yard on defenders who didn't have that same reading or knowledge of each others games, it just came naturally.

Who was the best player you played with?

David Speedie. I've played with some great players, people like Robson, Barnes, Hoddle, and Shilton. They were great, but Speedie was the most compatible for me in my time. All those other players were great as well though, but you can't compare a great goalie like Shilton, to a great striker like Speedie.

You talk about your compatibility with Speedie. A lot of people say you were never given a fair crack of the whip in terms of building up an understanding with the likes of Gary Lineker, and if you had, there's a fair chance you would have built up a relationship similar to the one you had with Speedie.

It was a dream come true for me when I was picked for the England squad in the first place, and then to actually play. I came on as a sub against Mexico in a pre-World Cup tour in 1985, after finishing joint top-scorer in the First Division with Gary Lineker.

It was an absolute pleasure to win my first full cap in the next game against West Germany in the Aztec Stadium. We won 3-1 and I scored twice, it was a dream debut. I spoke earlier about great moments like scoring at Arsenal, but if you talk about highlights, scoring on your debut for England would have to be an incredible high for a boy that was turned down twice, and told by good respected managers that he wouldn't make the grade.

How aware were you before you were called up, that England were coming to games and watching you?

There was constant speculation in the papers. Is he good enough? Isn't he good enough? You've got ex-players saying somebody else is better, it's all about opinions, and still is now. When I was around, there were another 15 or so strikers that played for England, the Mariner's, the Stein's, the Wright's, the Bright's, the Cottee's, the Harford's, the Bull's, the Lineker's, the Fashanu's, they all played for England.

All these players were playing for various teams when I was playing. I look today, and feel that players should be more proud to wear the shirt. When players pull out of internationals due to injury, and then play on a Saturday, it kills me, there's no pride in playing for England now. The support that goes with England is fantastic, and I loved it.

Can you remember where you were, and how you heard about your first England call-up?

I was at training, and John Hollins called me in the office. He said: "They've announced the England squad and you're in it, congratulations". I said thanks, I didn't go overboard about those things, I wasn't that sort of guy, but inwardly I felt brilliant. But all it was, was another hurdle I'd overcome.

I'd made the England squad, and now I had to go train with them, get myself in the team, and when I was in the team, I had to prove I could do it at that level. It was the next hurdle; a door was opening if you like.

When people talk about Kerry Dixon in an England shirt, they mainly remember the game against West Germany. You scored two, and laid on a third for Bryan Robson. What do you remember about the game?

I was nervous, the hairs stood up on the back of my neck, and my body was a tingle when I heard the national anthem. I was standing there, and I thought, Kerry Dixon, Chelsea and England.

What do I remember about the game? It was hot; it was about acclimatization for the World Cup in 1986. Glenn Hoddle played a ball in, and I chested it down for Bryan Robson to score, they then equalised. After that I scored a couple. Terry Butcher burst from the halfway line, and I was always quite quick. I got up with him and stayed onside. I screamed for him to pass, but Butch tried to go around the keeper, who touched it into my path.

I dug it out from under my feet, and watched agonizingly as it trickled in. It was heading for the post, but luckily for me it went in, as it was an open goal, it was an amazing feeling.

What do you remember about the pass for Robbo's goal?

Glenn Hoddle's ball was perfect, as it always was, Robbo's run and finish.......You look at modern day players, Lampard and Robson are very similar, his run and finish were good, I just had to make sure I did my part, the chest down, it was a good goal. The best goal for me was the header. The ball came across from Barnesey; I rose above two German defenders and headed it in.

Was you a particularly nervous player for club games?

I think it helps to have some nerves. You hope to do well in the big games; you want to play in them. If you go in there all casual and relaxed.....I'm generally a relaxed person, I know if I miss one or two chances, I'd be going all out to make sure I scored the third. I'm confident in my own ability, but there was always that bit of nerves.

Players could go out there with the best will in the world, having prepared right, but you might not have a good game, and there's other times when you don't do things right, and all of a sudden things start falling for you.

How did you used to psyche yourself up?

You just do it inwardly. You know what's coming. When I used to play against Tony Adams, he was the best defender I ever played against, and you think, I'm going to have to play well this weekend, don't drink too much, all those things. It didn't always work, but it just builds up as the game gets closer.

Was you a superstitious player?

I was one of the worst. If I'd scored in the game before, I'd do anything, walk out fourth, hold a ball, literally anything. I kept the same tie-ups for four years, they were rotten but they'd served me well and I was still scoring goals. Shin-pads I wore for about eight years, always wanted to keep the same type of boots. I had every superstition going. Even when I had a bad run, I decided to have a hair-cut or do something different, too many superstitions to remember.

What are your favourite Bobby Robson memories, and did he get your name right?

Well, there weren't too many Kerry Dixon's about. Bobby is a revered man; I'll never have a bad word said about him. He gave me my eight England caps; he's had a wonderful career and is arguably one of the greatest England manager's ever.

What do you remember about travelling with the squad to the 1986 World Cup?

It was wonderful. People said I wouldn't get picked because I had an injury that I picked up against Liverpool. I didn't play for over two months, and when I came back I only scored two goals. I wasn't playing well, and I wasn't as sharp as before.

I didn't have time on my side, but Don Howe came to watch me up at Man-Utd, and I scored twice in a 2-1 win. Bobby Robson later told me that was the game that got me in the squad, I thought it might have been. I only got on for six minutes in the World Cup, for Lineker against Poland. He was guaranteed to start, and it was between me and Peter Beardsley as to who would replace Mark Hateley, who hadn't done too well in the games previous.

Peter got the nod and I was on the bench. Luckily for England, Gary scored a hat-trick, and the Beardsley / Lineker partnership went on to be very fruitful for England. I was always going to be a sub, and I travelled with England for another year. I got a game against Sweden that we lost 1-0, and I wasn't in great form as Chelsea were struggling at the time under John Hollins. I got left out of the next squad, and never played for England again, but I've got some great memories, I saw Diego Maradona play first-hand, he was an amazing player.

How did the players feel after the 'hand of god' incident?

Peter Shilton knew immediately. He was complaining, and from where we were watching the game up in the boxes, we knew something was wrong. Nobody was sure until afterwards, it was sad but it was done.

Did you find it frustrating as a player, to be left on the bench?

It wasn't too often at Chelsea, more at the end of the Hollins era. For that part I was lucky and privileged in that I was regarded as a first-choice player. Sometimes it happens. Everyone at some point spends some time on the bench, that's inevitable and it's not easy. Some players are just happy to be part of the squad. I'd never be happy just to sit on the bench, I'd want to play. If I'm not in the team, I'd fight for my place.

Are you a fan of the rotation system that seems to be popular nowadays?

I'm a believer in rotation if it's necessary. I don't believe in rotating players if they're playing well. If I score a hat-trick, and there's another striker on the bench, I expect to keep my place. You fight for the right to get in the team, then you play well, coming in and out of the side doesn't help continuity, and it doesn't help getting to know your strike partners and your wingers, how they play, and where to make runs etc.

You look at the great Liverpool sides of the past, and they had five or six great players who played every week. Dalglish, Keegan and Toshack always played if they were fit. Look at Chelsea's great side from recent times. The main players should stay in the side if they're playing well.

When you look back at your Chelsea career now, what stands out as the highlight?

The amount of goals I scored, finishing where we did in the league on two occasions (5th and 6th). The highlight in terms of the fans, was the '94 cup semi-final at Wembley, when I was playing for Luton against Chelsea, and the Chelsea fans made their feelings known to me after the game.

It became the most emotional day of my life in terms of football, when they sung my name after Chelsea beat Luton 2-0, it was an amazing feeling, something I'll never forget.

How would you describe your relationship with the Chelsea fans?

I think it's very good. They've always treated me well, and still do. It's a case of me having time for them when I was a star, and they treat me as such now. It's great they never forget, and something that certain players will achieve and certain players won't.

How would you compare Chelsea fans with other supporters?

I'm sure other clubs have heroes, legends, and people they revere in the same way. Some people like you, some don't. Some people know you better, some don't. At the end of the day, have a bit of time and respect for people, and you'll probably get the same back.

Who did you room with at Chelsea?

I was there for nine years, and it was Joe McLaughlin for four or five years until he left, then it was David Lee, and for the last three years it was Dennis Wise.

Any funny stories about Wisey?

Loads, but they can't go on tape Dave. There was a few, he's a good friend of mine.

Were you surprised to see him leave Leeds and go up to Newcastle?

Yes, but I fully understand why. It was a job where he could live more in London and commute. He's based around the M25, and he could still do what he needed to do. It's a job for Dennis where he's not in the spotlight, and I think he wants a few years out of it perhaps.

How close was you to joining Arsenal?

Very close. Ken Bates actually stopped it. John Hollins told me I could go, he'd agreed terms with West-Ham and Arsenal. I spoke to John Lyall and George Graham, but I hadn't heard from Chelsea that Ken Bates was prepared to let me go.

I got summoned to see Batesey at Beaconsfield Farm, and he said: "Look, I don't know what's been going on, but you're not going, I want you to stay, I'm offering you a two year contract". He told me the manager would be going soon, but to keep it to myself, and sure enough, that's what happened.

When you look back at that episode, are you pleased with the outcome?

Absolutely. That was the outcome I wanted, I wanted to stay. I've got to say, Ken Bates was always alright for me. People give him a lot of stick, but Chelsea wouldn't be what it is now without the 20 years Ken had at the helm, and he will always be an integral part of their history.

How aware of Bobby Tambling's record were you when you were scoring all those goals at Chelsea?

I wasn't aware early on, but as the marks ticked by, the 100, the 150, I was in second place. The fans and I thought I'd break it, but the last season at Chelsea wasn't productive in terms of goals. Ian Porterfield was the manager, and it wasn't a great season. We had some good players, but I had a little falling out with Batesey, and Porterfield kept messing around with the team, it was a strange time.

I was told during the summer I wouldn't be playing for Chelsea again. They'd accepted an offer from Southampton. I was nine short of the record, and I thought I'd get it the next year, but being told I wasn't going to be given the opportunity to break it, I thought I'd move, and I went. They then signed Robert Fleck and Mick Harford, and if I'd known that, I would have stayed to fight for my place, but I wasn't to know, and that was it.

How much would it have meant to you to break Bobby's record?

It would have meant everything. Bobby Tambling was a lovely man. He did an amazing thing scoring all those goals for Chelsea, I should have broken it and I wish I had. It's the biggest footballing regret of my life, but it never happened. I'm a realist, and good luck to Bobby, I don't think it will ever be broken.

Someone from the age of 20-30, has to score 20 goals a season to get 200. That's why I gave Frank Lampard a standing ovation. For a midfielder to get over 100 goals…..Frank could come close if he signs a four-year contract, and he's a phenomenon for scoring goals.

How did the Southampton experience go?

It never went. Speedo had his normal row down the Isle of Wight with Terry Hurlock, which was all over the papers. He was there to partner me which never really happened. I had a back injury which kept me out for long spells; I only played 12 times, and scored two goals. I met some great guys down there. In terms of a club, it's a lovely club, but in terms of football, it never happened, and I jumped at the chance of going back to Luton when a loan move was offered.

David Pleat, who had kicked me out all those years ago, was the manager, and he needed a bit of experience up-front. When the loan move was offered, I took it, and it was an amazing feeling, coming back and playing for my hometown club. The cup run was amazing. I roomed with the late David Preece, who was a good friend of mine, a really nice guy. We had some good players, Paul Telfer, John Hartson, and people like Scott Oaks, who was the star of that cup run, we had lots of good players.

How did you feel about playing Chelsea in that semi-final?

We already knew, because we had to overcome West-Ham in a replay. We drew 0-0 at their place, and it was an amazing night at Kenilworth Road when we beat them 3-2. Scott Oaks scored a hat-trick, and with me knowing Chelsea awaited us at Wembley, it gave me extra impetus.

How would you have felt about scoring against Chelsea, and knocking them out?

I was a professional, and I wanted to get to a cup final. I only had one chance, and sadly we didn't perform as we had done, and Gavin Peacock scored two, and Chelsea went through. It wasn't a classic game, and sadly Luton disappointed on the day.

How did the move to Millwall come about?

David Pleat called me in one day and said that Mick McCarthy wanted me on loan at Millwall. He said: "Go down there and see how you get on. If you do well, they'll offer you a contract and extend your career." He pretty much said I wasn't going to get another deal at Luton, so I went. They had a decent side, including a German fella called Uwe Fuchs, and Chris Malkin, who were both ahead of me.

Some people were clapping me, but some were calling me a scummer. They didn't know whether to clap or cheer. We had some good honest players, and I gradually began to win the fans over, I think. Mick gave me a two-year deal in the summer which was amazing for me.

After Christmas the next season, Mick signed two Russians who were on huge money. One of them, Sergei Yuran, was a striker, and suddenly I wasn't getting in the side. Sadly I left the club. I was told Watford wanted me, which was a bit of a wrench. Being a Luton boy, Luton and Watford are rivals. However, it was close to home, and a two-year deal, and so I left. I was gutted that Millwall got relegated that same year.

How did the Watford fans react to you with your Luton background?

They hated me. They booed me before I'd even kicked a ball. I didn't play too much at Watford, I even had Luton fans asking me why I'd signed for them. As a footballer, I wanted to prolong my career. The reality is that you have to put food on the table I'm afraid.

It didn't last long, because Glenn Roeder, who had signed me, was sacked two or three games later, maybe signing me was the final nail in his coffin. Graham Taylor came in, and he gave me the opportunity to go to Doncaster as player-manager.

How aware are you of the crowd? Is it easy to pick out individual cries, and does it affect your game?

It ultimately could affect your game, but I'm too thick skinned for that. I used to get taunted at pretty much every away ground but it didn't matter, you become immune to it as a player, you just get on with it.

At Doncaster, how did you cope with the burden of being player-manager?

It was a burden because the Chairman / benefactor was used to running the side. I came in and got the players on my side, but the interference from the benefactor was incredible. If that's a side to football management, they are welcome to it. I'm a strong character, but he was over-bearing, and the club couldn't survive without him.

It was a scandalous situation, and it came to a head because I told the newspapers what was going on. There was uproar in the club, and it went into administration. I met some wonderful people at the club, and I think I'll always be welcome up there for exposing what was going on. For the good of the club, John Ryan took over, and it was a blessing when he bought the club.

Has that experience put you off the idea of management?

It didn't put me off. I went non-league for two years with Boreham-Wood, then went on to Letchworth, and Dunstable. I now ply my trade in other areas such as football punditry, commentary, and media work generally. I think management has passed me by now, and I like to think if I'd been given a chance, I'd have done alright.

Chelsea came along and offered me various roles. I'm now doing the hospitality there, and I'm involved with Chelsea TV, so that's where my future lies until someone comes along and offers me something else.

Who's the best manager you ever worked with?

John Neal. From the point of view that he signed me for Chelsea. Maurice Evans was great, I loved him. People who had faith in me got the best out of me; I was always determined to repay that faith.

Who's the funniest character you ever played with?

That's a tough call. Ian Dowie springs to mind, he's a funny guy. Andy Townsend had some great one-liners, Dennis Wise, David Speedie, all characters. Perry Groves was a funny guy as well. Football dressing-room's are generally about having a laugh.

You played with Terry Hurlock at Southampton, what was he like?

Terry's still a good friend. He was a great guy. Him and Speedo had their clash, and it was quite a hairy moment, I still see him socially and he's a great character.

What were the toughest away grounds to play at?

The toughest grounds for me, were the grounds we never won at. Chelsea had a poor record at Leeds, though I scored there for Southampton, so Elland Road was tough. The Old Den was a fearful place to visit, but I had good memories of a hat-trick there on the final day of the season in 1990.

Do you like getting recognised and being asked for your autograph?

It's nice that people still ask. If people choose to ask me for an autograph, I'm always willing to give it.

Do you keep in touch with your old team-mates?

Every now and again I see them. I'm not one for ringing up all the time, never have been, but I speak to some of the players.

What else do you like doing these days, outside your media work?

I play for Chelsea veterans, try to keep fit to a degree. I have a decent life, but I'm always looking for more work. I want to continue to watch Chelsea, and have an involvement in some capacity, but who knows what's around the corner.

Last question. How would Kerry Dixon like to be remembered?

Fondly. That's pretty much it. If people remember me for being a nice guy that will be enough.

Kerry Dixon

Ron Harris

Nobody has played more games in a Chelsea shirt. The man they call "Chopper"

How does it feel to be a Chelsea legend?

I do the hospitality here at Chelsea, I'm always looked after here, the people I work with are superb, and it gives me a thrill that I come here and people still recognise me. I sign autographs, and I feel very proud that I'm still associated with the club. To be classed as a legend is very special

Who, or what, inspired you to become a footballer?

My father was always keen. We used to support Arsenal, and I say to people, before I came to Chelsea, I was a 'Gooner'. I used to live in Hackney, and we'd go and watch Arsenal every week. We used to live in a place called Ravensdale Road, and where everybody used to have lovely flowerbeds, we just had a lawn; me, my brother Alan, and my dad, were just continually playing football and cricket, and I had the chance to take up cricket for a living.

Everybody had lovely gardens, and we just had posts. Me and Alan were out there for hours on end, and it was always my ambition to either play football if I was good enough, or even cricket. As I progressed, I had to make a decision whether to go to Chelsea, or even go to Lords for the cricket.

When did you first realise you would be able to make a living from football?

I was always playing against kids that were older than me. The teacher who took us for football at school was a lady. I was playing in the Under-11s at seven years of age, and I say to people, when I came on the staff at Chelsea, the junior teams were Under-18s, and I was only 15; it teaches you good things, because you're playing against older people that are more physical, and you get knocked about.

In those days, I'd imagine there was a considerable size difference. Did you still have the same tactics, was you still a hard player?

Funnily enough, I'm 5,8 and I used to play inside-right. It was only when I was in the youth team at Chelsea, and they had a fantastic youth policy, the players that came through were superb. Not being flash, but I went and trained at Spurs, West-Ham, Arsenal, and the one good thing about Chelsea, and West-Ham to be fair, was that if you was good enough at the age of 17, they would give you an early opportunity to play in the first team, and then it would be down to your ability.

We used to train at the *Welsh Harp* at Hendon, and the youth team manager was a fella called Dickie Foss, and he made me into a left-half. It was only after a while that I started to become a defensive left-half; basically, I used to stay back, and what I was good at when I first came into the side, and Tommy Docherty helped me with the aggression, was my concentration. I was very good at man-marking, I used to follow people around, the likes of Dennis Law and Jimmy Greaves; I'm proud of the fact that I played against Jimmy on about 20 odd occasions, and he only ever scored once.

How did you first hear that Chelsea were interested in signing you?

What I think swayed it, was that my brother came down here training a couple of years before me, and I used to be a ball-boy here when I was 12. I think if Alan had gone to West-Ham or Arsenal, I would have followed him, because we were a very close family. I think as soon as Alan liked the set-up here, it was inevitable that I was going to follow him to Chelsea.

What did you know about Chelsea before you joined the club?

Only from what Alan told me, that a lot of the lads were home-grown players, and as you get a bit older, you know at Chelsea you're going to be given a chance. I think apart from Alan coming here that's what swayed me.

What were your first impressions of the club after you'd signed?

It was very homely. The chief scout was a fella called Jimmy Thompson; he spotted the likes of 'Greavsie', and you always got well looked after. When I was a ball-boy, if Chelsea had an important game, they would invite me and my parents to come and watch, and they would give you the five-star treatment. They probably did it at every club at the time, but you were always made to feel welcome here.

How do you recall your first season?

It's very difficult. Bearing in mind I was 15, playing against lads that were 18, and who could be 6,2 the South East Counties was a good league. Chelsea would always do quite well, but it was quite physical, and playing up at the *Welsh Harp*, the wind would be really strong, and you'd be ankle-deep in mud.

You had to be quite fit to play, but I found it hard at first, adjusting from schoolboy football, but once you find your feet, then you progress, and by the time I was 17, I'd moved from youth football to reserve football. I remember the first game I played for the reserves; I played with about eight internationals, and we had gates of 10,000 people.

What do you remember about your first-team debut?

I was very nervous to start with. Chelsea weren't doing particularly well; they were rock bottom at the time. The lads were very good though, they tried to make you feel confident, I remember going to bed early the night before, and dreaming that I was going to have a good game. We were playing against Sheffield Wednesday, and they had some really good players.

As I say, I was nervous, we won 1-0 I think, but it's quite daunting playing in front of 40,000. I had played at Wembley for England schoolboy's in front of 100,000, but now I was playing for my living. We did quite well, and I remember Tommy Docherty telling me to make sure I won the ball if it was there to be won. I marked a lad called Johnny Fanton, and Tommy put his arm around me afterwards and said: "Well done, terrific", and I was quite proud, I thought I'd done quite well

The following week we went up to Everton and got beat 6-0. I didn't play regularly again until the following season, but Tommy must have seen something in me, because he made me captain of the side at an early age.

How did it feel to get a taste of first-team football, and then be playing with the reserves again?

I always tell young kids that you start off at the bottom of a ladder. You're in the junior side, and then you have to do a little bit more to get in the reserves. Once you get into the reserves, you have to improve a little bit more, in order to make the first-team, and then when you're in the first-team, you can't relax, you have to put in that bit extra to stay in the side.

After Chelsea were relegated, I came into the team, and I played regularly until Danny Blanchflower took over, I don't think I was ever dropped. Then Eddie McCreadie took over, and he brought in a lot of youngsters, which led to some of the older players being pushed into the reserves. If you do get put in the reserves, you have a choice; you can either sulk, which does nobody any good, or you can roll your sleeves up and go like leather.

What was your most memorable game in a Chelsea shirt?

Many years ago we beat Leicester 1-0. I hadn't been in the side long, and we had a player called Frankie Blunstone; he was a good player, but very selfish. Leicester had

37

Gordon Banks in the side, and Frankie cut a ball back to me, which I hit from 30 yards into the top corner, so that was a good feeling.

Also, I remember getting to the 1967 cup final. It was the first all-London cup final, and I remember Tommy Docherty saying he'd played in a Preston side that got beat by West Brom. He told us we'd achieved something by being in the final, and it was true, even though we got beat.

Three years later, we played in another cup final against Leeds, and I was the first Chelsea player to lift the FA Cup, so the two cup finals stand out in my career.

You mentioned your goal against Gordon Banks. What was the best goal you ever scored?

I remember scoring against West-Ham in a 5-5 draw, and I sliced a ball past Peter Bonetti into my own goal. We went straight up the other end, and I hit a fantastic volley to make it 5-5, that was one hell of a goal.

How would you describe the feeling of scoring a goal?

It's funny because people react differently. You watch people today taking their shirts off, but to be truthful, I just used to turn around and salute the lads, go from there.

More familiar territory now Ron, what was your favourite tackle?

In the '70 cup final replay, myself and Dave Webb swapped positions, and as much as Dave got all the accolades for scoring the winning goal, I thought I deserved a pat on the back for a tackle I did on Eddie Gray after about eight minutes. I've seen Eddie on a few occasions, and he's a good lad. I remember about two years ago, he came up to me, and gave me a stud, he said: "They've just taken that out of my knee, I think it's yours", but he's a good lad.

Also, I did a tackle on George Best; he rode the tackle, but people always remember it because it was one of the clips they used to show on *Grandstand*, even now when I see it, I always think I'm going to tackle him.

Who did you enjoy kicking the most?

Anybody that moved. Without being disrespectful to anybody in today's game, football today is a non-contact sport. Years ago you had the likes of Tommy Smith and Norman Hunter; they were aggressive players, and the aggression has been taken out of football nowadays.

Is there anyone in today's game that you'd like to kick?

Cristiano Ronaldo. I think I might make him swap wings.

What did you enjoy more, a match-winning goal, or a match-saving tackle?

I didn't score many goals, but my job was to defend. Full-backs today are more like wingers, they like to get forward, but half of them can't defend to save their lives. We were taught how to defend properly, and you see some of these so-called world class players, and they're good on the ball, but my job was to stop you from scoring, and try to rough you up a bit.

Who was the best manager you played under?

I've always found it very difficult to divide Dave Sexton and Tommy Docherty. Tommy was a fantastic motivator of players. Coaching was non-existent in my time, and we didn't know what it was all about until Dave came down. I remember him coming down one day with all these bollards; he'd put them yards apart all over the pitch, and that's how we would practice zonal marking. We used to spend hours on the training pitch and it was fantastic, I thought they were both great managers though, I've always said that.

Who was the most overrated hard-man you played against?

There used to be some tough fellas. I played for the Football League against the Scottish League, and there was a guy playing for us called John McGrath. Just before we went out, he took a giant swig of whiskey; I'd never seen that before. There used to be a fella called Dennis Hollywood at Southampton, Jimmy Gabriel, they were all tough players.

I'll tell you who used to always have a moan-up, Martin Peters. He never used to stop moaning if anybody went near him, he was a nice enough fella though. If you look at more modern football, take Paul Ince for example; what did they call him? 'Guvnor'. Well, I would have liked to see him play with some of the tough guy's years ago. Alan Mullery had a bit of a reputation for being a tough guy, but I don't think he was, he might have been tough outside of football, but not on the pitch.

You spoke about Martin Peters, and the fact he didn't like being harassed. When you knew that, did it make you do it even more?

You used to look at the team sheet before a game to find out who you'd be marking, and with certain players, you knew that one good tackle would be enough. There was a fella at Man City, Peter Barnes, and when you gave him a few verbals he'd move over to the other wing.

Were there any opposition players that you were scared of?

No, I'm not the biggest of fellas, and I've never had a fight off the field, but on the field I'd back myself to beat anybody when it came to a 50-50. My dad instilled into me the belief that you get nothing for coming second; he told me to make sure I won the ball, and then to give it to players like Alan Hudson or Charlie Cooke, who could make things happen.

What do you make of the current generation of so-called hard players, the likes of Robbie Savage etc?

Well, we talk about Terry Hurlock. Now let me tell you, if you threw a ball between Terry Hurlock and Robbie Savage, there would only be one winner, and it wouldn't be Robbie Savage. We're talking about some real tough geezer's in my time, when football was played by men.

People mention Vinnie Jones, but in his time he was probably the only tough fella about. It's like being at school; if you know somebody has a reputation for giving people a good hiding, you wouldn't go and pick on him would you?

Do you think there's a place in today's game for the so-called hard man?

I don't see any reason why not, but nowadays you get penalised for slide tackles that would have been fine in my day.

Amazingly, considering your style of play, you had quite a good disciplinary record.

I got sent-off once. I'll be the first to admit, I kicked a few people, but I never hit anybody. We played Brighton in a league-cup tie, and we were winning 2-0 with ten minutes to go. They had a player called Eddie Spearitt, who gave me a few verbals. Well, they were in Division 4 at the time, so I told him he'd like to be paying more tax every week, and pushed him away; he fell on the floor and rolled around a bit, so I got sent-off.

The system was different back then though, because you could appeal. I got banned for three matches, and appealed it. There was a fella at the game, a Brighton fan, and he was a vicar; he wrote a lovely letter, saying he thought Spearitt had made a meal out of it, and the ban got reduced to one match.

What was your relationship like with the official's off the pitch?

If you look at my disciplinary record, I only ever got booked for tackles, or reckless tackles. I can't see the point in calling a referee all the names under the sun, because if you book me for that, or book me for kicking somebody, it's the same punishment, and I'd rather hurt somebody than give a ref verbals.

Which modern-day footballer would you most compare yourself to?

Obviously the lad here, John Terry. He came through the youth ranks, like I did, he's captain, like I was, he lacks a yard of pace, which I did, but the big difference between me and John Terry, is that when I tackled, the forward never got up.

How did the Stamford Bridge atmosphere affect your game?

I've always had a fantastic relationship with the fans here, and people are understanding towards those who try. I played under seven managers here, and one thing I wasn't, was a cheat or a spiv. From me, the manager's got 110 per cent, week in, week out, on the training field, and on a Saturday. I think the supporters saw that, and it was against my pride to lie down if I was injured, I think I only ever got carried off once.

What went through your mind when the crowd sung your name?

It's a fantastic feeling. If we played away and people booed me, it was because either we were winning, or big players weren't doing well. I've had good and bad games, and I've always had a great relationship with the Chelsea fans, I love coming down here.

How do Chelsea fans compare to other club's supporters?

I think the best supporters in the country for atmosphere, are at Anfield. Even when we used to go up there, they were very appreciative when the teams came out; they don't boo you like they do at Old Trafford, but I think the supporters at Chelsea are superb. When we went to Athens, the replay was two days later, and they ended up staying overnight and things like that, they're the true supporters.

What was the most intimidating away ground in those days?

Leeds was never the most popular place; there's always been great rivalry between us. Millwall was another one. I didn't play there too often, but I remember playing there in the London Challenge Cup; all the big sides played their reserves, and the Old Den was a very intimidating place.

Who did you enjoy playing against most?

I used to relish playing against Arsenal, with me being an Arsenal supporter; it was always a full-house, and we always did well over there. They used to do quite well here, but we always did well over there, and being that I used to live not far away, I always enjoyed it.

Which player was your toughest opponent?

I've always said to people, the toughest player I ever played against was a big Scottish fella called Andy Lockhead. If you speak to the likes of Norman Hunter, and Tommy Smith, what they used to love to do, was get in early, and clatter somebody. The player would normally get a bit jumpy, and then you knew you had them in your pocket. With Andy Lockhead though, if you went in early, ten minutes later, you'd get exactly the same back. Ability wise, he wasn't tremendous, but he was a big, strong guy, and he was a nuisance.

Who was the best player you played with?

I've always said Peter Osgood. He was the most gifted player I played with; superb touch, scored fantastic goals, he could play, but he could also look after himself, he was a good lad.

You mentioned Jimmy Greaves only scored once against you in 19 games. What was your secret?

I used to get in early, hassle him, and I used to follow him everywhere. When I first started playing against these players, Tommy Docherty said to me: "If he goes to the toilet, follow him", and Jimmy used to look at me, and say: "Are you still with me 'Chopper'?" He was the greatest goalscorer in the country, but I think I had the upper-hand with him.

What do you remember about the time when you became club captain at Chelsea?

Tommy Docherty and Terry Venables had a falling out, and Terry left. Tommy just said to me one day: "You're captain of Chelsea." I was over the moon because I was only 20.

Can you remember anybody giving you any advice that stands out?

No, any manager I worked with at Chelsea would back me 100 per cent, if I saw fit to make a change during the game. They would sometimes come in and say: "Why did you do that?", because they could see things from the stands that I couldn't see. Nobody ever queried me if, for example, if I pushed 'Webby' further up with 20 minutes to go.

How did your nickname 'Chopper' come about?

From the Chelsea supporters. They used to say I'd scythe people down from behind, and the name just stuck. People never call me Ron though, it's always: "Hello 'Chopper', how are you?"

How would you feel if John Terry suddenly developed the name, and you had to share it with him?

I'd say to him: "There's only one 'Chopper', and that's me.

I know a few of your team-mates called you 'Buller'.

Yes, 'Ossie' used to call me that, because he reckoned I spoke so much bullshit it wasn't true.

Do you agree with him?

To a degree, yes. Ha ha

Who had the biggest influence on you as a player?

The few occasions I went to Arsenal and saw Duncan Edwards, the Man Utd player who was killed in the Munich air disaster. I used to think he was a superb player because he could play, he was aggressive, and I think he was a good role-model for any young lad.

What did you say to Ray Wilkins when he took over the captaincy from you?

That was the manager's decision, and it was entirely up to him. Ray will tell you, I was the first to go up to him; I don't hold grudges, and it was Eddie McCreadie's decision. I played occasionally when Ray was captain, but that was when I was sub most of the time. Obviously I was disappointed, but that's life.

You are without doubt, the most famous Chelsea captain. What qualities make a good captain?

You have to set a good example on and off the pitch. Don't get me wrong, I've had a few drinks as much as anybody else, but if I was told to be in by 12, I would be. I was seldom injured; sometimes I'd play with a bit of pain, just setting an example. If you look at John Terry here, somebody who throws himself into last ditch tackles, the players respect that.

In the years I was captain, I knew that if I went up to Charlie Cooke for example, and had a go at him, he would sink even lower. Somebody like 'Ossie', who could be a bit lazy, if you gave him a kick up the arse, you'd get a bit more from him. After a while you knew how to handle the players, and I think they respected me for what I was.

How do you think the current team compares to the team which won the cup-winners-cup in 1970-71?

Football's changed completely. You can't really compare, and don't get me wrong, the current side's record speaks for itself over the last few years, but the side we had was a very good side.

You've played alongside some Chelsea greats. What's your favourite Peter Osgood memory?

I remember him as a young lad, he wasn't even 18, and we played up at Burnley. He ran from the halfway line, and beat four or five players, before scoring; that was one of the best goals I saw him score. He was out for a long time with a broken leg at one point, and when he came back, he scored two great goals; one against AC Milan, and the other against a German side, but the one at Burnley was one of the best I saw him score.

You also played a lot of games with Peter Bonetti. What's your favourite memory of Peter?

As a defender, you liked your keeper to be very confident, and we knew Peter had the ability to come out and catch balls, he wasn't one for staying on his line, Peter. There was nothing of him, he must have only weighed 11st, but he was very good at coming for crosses. His worst attribute was that he couldn't kick a ball, he was hopeless at kicking.

Who did you room with?

For years I roomed with Marvin Hinton. As soon as he came from Charlton, we were room-mates for years until we parted company.

Any good memories stand out?

Yes, he was one of the lads who got sent home from Blackpool. We used to call him 'One arm Lou'. There used to be a ticket tout with that name, and Marvin used to go and knock a few tickets out, so that's what we used to call him.

You spoke about the famous away game at Burnley.

That was the closest Chelsea ever came to winning the title in that era. There was only Man Utd, Leeds, and ourselves, and if you ask Tommy Docherty, he'd tell you that if the same thing happened today, he would have done things differently; he acted on impulse, and he felt let down.

I remember him telling the lads that he'd see them at breakfast, and when they came down, he gave them their train tickets and told them the train left at 10.30. We got beat at Burnley 6-1, or 6-2, and then he brought them all back the following week. There was only a few weeks to go, and I think losing them points cost us the title really.

Terry Venables was said to have been a popular figure in the Chelsea dressing-room. How do you recall your relationship with him?

Terry was one of these fellas, and I think Tommy sussed him out after a period of time. Terry wanted to run the whole show, and he had a big sway with the players here. I think there was a bit of animosity between the two of them, and it was inevitable that they would part company. I got on alright with Terry, but I think when he lost the captaincy, our relationship drifted, because I took over from him.

Is it true that you're friends with Sir Elton John?

My wife used to work for a music publisher's called *Dick James Music*, and Elton John was an office boy, he didn't have a pot to piss in at this point, we used to call him 'Silly Reg'. I saw him a few years ago at Watford and he still remembers us. I used to spend hours up there, because I started courting my Mrs, and he was always there, but he'll always say to me: "How's Lee?", which is what they called my Mrs, but her real name is Lynn. I went to a game at QPR, and he was there, and he came over and asked how she was. I wouldn't say he was a down and out, but he was a nobody. Then he went and made a fortune, but I do like him, he's a fantastic singer, brings back old memories.

What's the funniest request you've had from a fan?

Funniest request

Mmmm

I heard a rumour that one of them tried to tell you how to tackle.

No, that was Dario Gradi. He came down here from the FA to do a coaching course, I think somebody left, and he took over the running of the reserve side. Dave Sexton was away one day, and we had a practice game. Two things happened; he had a pop at Marvin Hinton. Marvin wasn't an aggressive player, he was about 5,11 but not that commanding in the air, and he came up to Marvin and said: "You don't head the ball properly", and Marvin said: "I've been a pro' for ten years so I haven't done badly". He then turned to me and said: "You don't tackle properly", so I said: "I'm quite pleased with the way I tackle", and left it at that really.

You've always enjoyed a good rapport with the fans at Chelsea, although one occasion does stand out, when you played against Stoke, and Stanley Matthews.

Yes, I think that's the first time I ever got a bit of stick. Stan was 49 then, and I'd just turned 17. Me and Eddie McCreadie tried to rough him up a bit, and he did love a moan, Stan. I think they played on it a bit; it was his last game, in London, and he was retiring. He did a lap of honour when they came out, and I think the crowd had a bit of sympathy. I think that's the only time I had a bit of stick from the supporters.

Most Chelsea fans struggle to remember a time when you were on the pitch injured. What was your secret?

Years ago people played with pain. I can remember colliding with the goalkeeper, John Phillips, and I was coughing up blood. The doctor said I'd have to go to hospital, but I wanted to wait until after the game. It finished up that I cracked my ribs.

Another time, up at York, I needed eight stitches, because a geezer caught me on the bone. At that time you didn't get injections, so the doctor put these stitches in, my eye was getting smaller and smaller, and he told me I couldn't go back out, but I went back out and played for another 45 minutes.

Some people play with pain, and some don't, fortunately enough, I could. People say now about a metatarsal; well years ago, a metatarsal was a broken toe, and people played with broken toe's, they would put a bit of cotton wool around it, and it only hurt if somebody trod on it.

I had injections before the 1970 cup final. I couldn't even jog on the Thursday, so Dave asked me if I wanted to take a gamble, and of course I did. I couldn't walk afterwards, and that's why I came off before extra-time, I hadn't trained for a month.

Speaking of the cup final, what's your greatest memory of the day itself?

The whole day from when you wake up is fantastic. You've got all the press people around, we had the local barber come down to do all our hair, then you have the pre-match meal, and you get the police escorting you up Wembley way. So the day itself, leading up to kick-off is fantastic.

How did the team celebrate lifting the trophy?

After the replay, we went out on the piss in Manchester. We had a little dinner beforehand, then we went clubbing it; I remember getting back to Euston, and going on an open-top bus tour around Chelsea, stopping at the town hall where they had a reception for us.

I tell people that I was very privileged to captain a great bunch of lads. If somebody asked one of us to go and visit a sick child in hospital, ten players would want to go, they were great lads. The back four could have a kick and a dig, then you had the ball players, and then 'Ossie' and 'Hutch' up-front. As much as the ball players needed us, we needed them as well.

Bearing in mind you had such a great relationship with the FA Cup; does it sadden you to see so many teams downgrade it nowadays?

I can remember winning the Milk Cup years ago, and that was a major competition, but you have youth players playing in that these days. The FA Cup has been devalued over the years, because even some of the Premiership teams play a fringe side. Half the time, they're just looking to stay in the Premiership.

Do you have any regrets about your international career?

People seem surprised when I say I never played for England. I captained the youth side, and the Under-23s, but if I picked my best Chelsea 11, and you picked yours, we would all differ. Maybe the people in charge at the time didn't rate me. To be truthful, I'm proud of my career, but it would have been nice just to get one cap, but it wasn't to be.

Had Scotland or Ireland come knocking, would you have been tempted to get the family tree out?

Not really. I was born and bred a cockney, and I don't believe in all that. It's like Vinnie Jones playing for Wales, I don't think it's right.

What was it like, playing in an era when England were world champions?

I think if you look at that era, if you had to pick a world 11, 'Banksy' would have always got in it, 'Mooro' would have always got in it, Bobby Charlton would have got in it, and I would think Jimmy Greaves. Not so much 'Hursty', because he wasn't really involved until the latter stages, but you had four players that would have walked in any world 11.

Now if you go through players over the last few years, I wouldn't think there are too many people that would get in a world 11. I think football's changed completely

What do you put that down to?

I think there are too many foreigners in our football; you've only got to look at the goalkeeping situation. Over the years, we've had some fantastic goalkeepers, I could name six or seven, and really, apart from the fella in goal at the moment who's having a bit of a crisis, David James is coming to the end of his career, people talk about the fella Green; who else is there? Not too many people. I think there are some fantastic young foreign players, but they should gradually cap it. Look at Arsenal; they seldom field an English player.

Are you tempted to have a word with Peter, see if he'll put his gloves back on?

He played the other week in that *Sky Sports* thing didn't he? He's getting a bit past it now though.

What sort of relationship did you have with the press during your career?

Fine. It's completely different nowadays, but they just used to wait outside the dressing-room, you could talk to them though, but you soon get to know the people that would drop you in the cart, so you had to be careful what you said; they have a knack of twisting things, but I always got on alright with them.

How do you think you would have coped today, with paparazzi camped outside your house?

I wouldn't mind it for £120,000 a week.

Today an average player is a multi-millionaire. Do you feel you were born in the wrong era?

I've had a fantastic time in football, and I think football in our day was more enjoyable than what it is today. We used to always stay in a hotel in London before a game, and we could go to the dogs on a Friday night. There used to be about eight of us go down to Wimbledon, as long as we were back in the hotel by the right time.

You weren't plastered on TV four or five days a week, and I don't think today's players have the lives we had, because they can't go out nowadays without people taking photos. People with young kids could come and watch us train, you could have a cup of tea with them, sign a few autographs, but nowadays you can't get anywhere near the training grounds.

What's the best compliment you've ever been paid by an opposing player or manager?

I don't know why, but every time we played against Nottingham Forest, Brian Clough would always be by the touchline, and whether we won or lost, he'd always come up to me and say: "Well done, son", and that's from one of the greatest managers.

At half-time when Chelsea were losing, how much could a manager do or say, to bring about an improvement in the second half?

We used to only get ten minutes, so the lads would have a quick cup of tea and sit down. He might change one or two positions, or try to motivate he players. People in the dug-out see things differently, and if he changes things and the team win, he's the best manager in the country, but if they don't, people knock him.

Do you recall any inspiring speeches, or roastings at half-time?

I've had a few roastings. Years ago here, somebody wrote in, I think his name was Paul Travillion, and it was one of those mind over matter things. Dave Sexton said to us, that instead of coming in at half-time, we had to stay out on the pitch. He told us to do some ball exercises; passing, throwing the ball to Peter Bonetti etc, so that when the other team came back out and saw what we were doing, they would think that we were really up for it. We tried it for a few weeks, and never won a game, so I went to see Dave, and told him it wasn't working.

What were your funniest memories at Chelsea?

The two comedians in the dressing-room were John Hollins and Eddie McCreadie. Eddie was funny, and John Hollins used to take off Tommy Cooper to a tee, if you closed your eyes, you'd have thought that John Hollins was Tommy Cooper. They were the two comedians, although other people had a few stories to tell.

Tommy Cooper coming down wouldn't have been as strange as it sounds, because you did have a few famous visitors didn't you?

We used to have Steve McQueen, Jimmy Tarbuck, and Arthur Askey. I don't think they were all Chelsea fans, I suppose some of them were, but they used to come and watch us, and then go and do their shows in the evening.

How popular was that with the players?

They never used to stay long. It wasn't an open house or anything.

We spoke a bit about how training changed under Dave Sexton. What sort of trainer were you?

I wasn't really that interested in coaching, although I did later spend three years at Brentford. It was Dave who started sending the lads on coaching courses, but I'm a great believer that I was born with a gift, and that gift was playing football.

Who was your favourite partner in the middle of the park?

I didn't really play that often at Brentford, but I played about 30 games with Terry Hurlock. A lot of people saw him come out with the long hair, and used to think he was somebody from a different planet. He could play though, and he was very tough, always an asset to have in your side.

Do you have any regrets when it comes to management?

It's nice if you're earning £3m a year, but you have to start somewhere. The problem is, when you get the bullet from Brentford or Aldershot, where do you go from there? If I'd started my managerial career at Arsenal, you can work your way down, but there are only 92 league clubs, so there can only be 92 managers.

Legend has it, that you had an opportunity to go back to Chelsea as a coach.

I was at a function when Ken Bates was chairman, and he did ask me if I'd like to come back here. I met him in a restaurant in Chelsea, and at the time they weren't doing very well. I was sitting there, thinking I was about to be offered the job, when Ken Bates walked in with John Neal, so I wasn't interested then. Shortly after, John Hollins was approached, and he took the job.

There was a bit of a row in the press between you and Ken Bates, what happened there?

I got a call one day from a guy at *The Sun*, asking me if I knew Dave Webb had been sacked. I told him I didn't, and then he asked me my thoughts, so I told him I thought Ken Bates had used 'Webby'. I then got a solicitor's letter saying my comments had caused distress to Ken and his family. In the end, *The Sun* paid £1100 to a charity of Ken's choice. He's not my flavour of the month, and I didn't come down here for almost ten years through that. It was only because all the lads did a reunion for Peter

Osgood, and the first person we bumped into was Ken Bates; he shook my hand and said: "Let's bury the hatchet", which we did, and that was that.

Do you still see the other lads?

Peter Bonetti works with me here, and I still see some of the lads. I try to get them involved in some of the functions we do, so I see some of them. We've got a big reunion coming up in April for a cancer charity.

What did you make of the Jose Mourinho years?

Chelsea have had three good years. They've won a few things, but like everything else, there will always be a Chelsea Football Club, with or without Jose Mourinho.

What advice would you give the current Chelsea players?

I think there is so much money involved today, not only at Chelsea, that you only have to sign a three-year contract at one of the better sides, and if you don't walk away a millionaire, you need locking up. Whereas in our time, I left here in 1980, and I was earning £295 a week, which was a lot of money then, but I think players today get better advice than we did. I'm not saying I did stupid things, but in any sport today, if you're successful, you can earn a fortune. I'm sure some of them won't be doing what I do; travelling up the motorway to do after-dinner speaking, because they won't want to do it.

If you were Chelsea manager now, with an unlimited transfer budget, who would you sign?

For quite some time here, they've lacked a Jimmy Greaves. If you take Drogba and Anelka out of the equation, there aren't too many people up-front that are regular goalscorers, and what Chelsea need is someone who will get them 20 goals every season. I know there are not too many people around, but in every other position they're fine. When Drogba missed three games, they scored once, and to put the icing on the cake, they need an out-and-out goalscorer.

Do you have any regrets about your playing career?

No, I've had 21 fantastic years here as a player, and like anything else, all good things come to an end.

What are you up to these days?

I do the hospitality here, and travel all around doing the after-dinner circuit. I'm quite happy with life; I've been married 39 years so I must be doing something right.

Last question. How would Ron Harris like to be remembered?

As somebody who gave 110 per cent, week in, week out, and done a good job for the seven managers that I served at Chelsea.

Peter Bonetti

Arguably Chelseas best ever goal keeper and also a member of the world-cup-winning squad from 1966

How does it feel to be regarded as a Chelsea legend?

I don't know how to take that at times. I feel flattered obviously, but I've never thought of myself as a legend. When we played football in our day, we were just footballers, we weren't superstars. Yes, we were in the public eye all the time, yes, we played in front of thousands of people every week, but we were just footballers. We enjoyed it, got paid for it, and we were the luckiest people alive. When you retire and people say you're a legend, I take it as a great compliment, but you know, what is a legend?

How did you come to sign for Chelsea?

My parents came from London, but I was living in Sussex at the time. I was playing for a local team and getting rave reports. I was only 15, and playing in the men's league, and I was always on at my dad about writing to Chelsea for a trial.

In those days, the network of scouting wasn't as vast as it is today. They had scouts in London, but as I was in Sussex, that didn't help me. My mum, in the end, wrote to Chelsea for a trial, and I got a letter back, saying they wanted me to go up one Saturday to where the Chelsea juniors trained, and I played in a game. I didn't have much to do in that game, so they invited me back again, and liked what they saw. They asked me to sign for the juniors, so I did.

Can you remember how you felt when you actually signed?

I was chuffed, as I hoped it was the first step on my way to being a footballer, but I never realised my career would go as well as it did.

What did you know about Chelsea before you joined?

It's funny, because Chelsea were one of the sides that were giving youngsters a chance. They had a great scout, a guy called Jimmy Thompson. He recruited a lot of London boys, the likes of Terry Venables, Ron Harris and Ken Shiletto. They had a very good youth system as well; Dick Foss was the manager, and they had great success bringing youngsters through, Jimmy Greaves being the shining example. They had a name for giving young boys a chance.

What were your first impressions of the club?

It was daunting at first; the lads used to give me a lot of stick as I wasn't from London. I had to travel up from Worthing, and it was a different world. We had a great team, and I started at Chelsea with Venables, Alan Harris, Bobby Tambling and Barry Bridges, to name a few.

Chelsea had the pick of the crop in those days, as they were winning the South East Counties league on a regular basis, and the first year I was there, we won the youth cup, we certainly had a good side.

How long did you have to wait for your debut?

In those days it was just pure luck. As in life, you need a bit of luck, and I was 18 when I ended up making my debut. I was doing well for the juniors, and Chelsea got two injuries. Reg Matthews was the goalkeeper at the time, and Bill Robertson was the back-up; both were internationals, for England and Scotland respectively, and we also had the England youth keeper, Barry Smart. He wasn't playing so well at the time, and Ted Drake called me into his office on the Thursday morning and told me he was going to give me a chance. As it turned out, I was playing for the juniors one week, and making my full Chelsea debut the next.

Do you recall how you felt?

I was surprised, and I remember telling Ted it was a great honour. On the day I was very nervous. I was a quiet lad in those days, and I was overawed by the whole occasion. We were playing Man City at Stamford Bridge, and as luck would have it, we won 3-0, and I stayed in for the rest of the season, that was the start of my career.

As a youngster, do you recall any bits of advice you were given by the senior pros at the time?

They gave me encouragement more than anything else. They couldn't really give me advice on goalkeeping, as they weren't goalkeepers, but they were very supportive; they gave me confidence by boosting me up prior to the game, and it was a great team harmony. In those days, the juniors and first-team trained separately, so I didn't see a lot of the senior players until I started playing with them.

What were your most memorable games in a Chelsea shirt?

There were so many; when you think I ended up playing 729 games for the club, a lot of games stood out. The games that stand out most though, are when you win things. When we won the FA cup in 1970, the first time Chelsea had won it, that was memorable because we actually won a medal for it.

We then won the cup winners cup the following year, beating Real Madrid. Prior to those triumphs, we had been a very consistent team; we never won the league, but for about ten years in a row, we finished in the top four or five, which is commendable.

What was your best save?

Every save was important, but saves made in the cup finals were more important because they helped us win the cup, so those are the ones that stand out in my mind.

How would you describe the feeling of pulling off a match-winning save?

It's part of your job, you don't really analyse it. A lot of the time you'll make a save, and you don't realise you've made such a good save because it's instinctive. It's pure reactions; when you're training day-in, day-out, and playing every week, you just react to situations, and when a shot comes in, hopefully you'll get to it.

Which team did you enjoy playing against the most?

The top teams. Liverpool at Anfield was always a special atmosphere, and in fairness to the kop, they were superb, they appreciated good goalkeepers. If you made a brilliant save, they would applaud it, and I enjoyed going up there, which is strange because I never won up there in the league, only in the cup.

What were the hardest away games?

Liverpool, Man Utd, and Leeds in those days were always strong. You could never underestimate any team though. I always looked on away games as a hard challenge, because if you get complacent, that's when you make mistakes.

How did the atmosphere at Chelsea affect your game?

I was lucky, in that I was different. Because I wasn't the biggest goalkeeper, I had to rely on my agility to make saves, and to perform. Most goalies in those days were big guys, and they were just stoppers; I relied on agility and reflexes. Because that was different, and I had a foreign sounding name, the fans took to me and gave me great encouragement. I was probably one of the first goalies to wave to the crowd, because they used to chant my name from the shed end.

The fans were unbelievable, and even to this day, I go and do the hospitality on match days at Chelsea, and the support from the fans is unbelievable. It's a wonderful compliment to have them respect and revere you. I got on very well with the fans, and it was wonderful.

How do Chelsea fans compare with those of other clubs?

Fans at all clubs are fanatics. The Anfield and Old Trafford fans were great for their own teams, although the Old Trafford faithful weren't so keen on opposing goalkeepers. You have to admire fans' loyalty, and the amount of travelling they do, whatever club they belong to. Even if you made a mistake, the Chelsea fans just accepted it and got behind you even more.

How much does the crowd's chanting affect your game as a goalkeeper?

You just hear murmurs really; the more noise that was at a ground, the more I liked it, and if the crowd started having a go at me, it would just spur me on to try even harder. If you're getting stick, it normally means that you're doing well. I'd like to think that I was a good professional, and as a goalkeeper, concentration levels were key; if you lose that concentration level, you'll give away silly goals. Sometimes you would hear things from the crowd, and you could only laugh, because you couldn't afford to let it get to you.

What's the strangest question you've ever been asked by a fan?

It's just the usual stuff really, what's your greatest save? What was it like playing in front of such big crowds? I just love talking to them to be honest. Even on holiday, you get people coming up to you, but I enjoy being recognised, and I like chatting about football, I've never refused people when they've wanted a chat.

Do you recall when you first picked up your nickname, 'the cat'?

Very much so. In those early days, the first-team had a striker called Ron Tindall, he played cricket for Surrey as well. We used to meet in the billiard room before the game to play darts or snooker. Tindall used to go around with a camera, giving a running commentary on what we were doing, and one day he referred to me as 'the cat', and it stuck. Even to this day people still use it, and I see it as a privilege and an honour.

What's the biggest compliment you've ever been paid, by an opposing player or manager?

I've heard of manager's telling their teams that they're playing against a top-class goalkeeper, and telling them that they need to be at their best, that sort of stuff. The fact they want to put me off my game is a big compliment.

Who's the best manager you ever worked under?

At club level, I would have to say Dave Sexton, because he was a great tactician, a great coach. He took over from Tommy Docherty, who had given all of us young boys our chance. Tommy was more volatile, that was just his way, whereas Dave was quieter, and Dave had more success in our era than any other manager.

At international level, I was fortunate enough to work under Alf Ramsey. I was in the world-cup-winning squad of 1966, but didn't play, as I was understudy to the great Gordon Banks. I was honoured to be involved at the time though, and Alf was without doubt, a great manager.

At half-time, if Chelsea were losing, how much could a manager say to bring about an improvement in the second half?

Quite a lot if he knew his tactics. Tommy would come in and rant and rave to get us wound up, he made you wake up if you weren't playing well. Dave would talk tactics to you, he might change the system slightly, or he'd notice what certain opposing players were doing to cause us problems, so he would try and rectify it. If they know their stuff they can certainly help you turn a game around.

Do you recall any major inspiring speeches?

The best tactical change Dave made was in the cup final against Leeds. In the first game at Wembley, Dave Webb played right-back, and he was marking Eddie Gray.

Well, Eddie had a blinder, and he was causing us real problems, so in the replay, Dave moved Ron Harris to right-back, and put Dave Webb in the middle. It worked tremendously, because Ron marked Eddie Gray out of the game, and 'Webby' went on to score the winning goal, so that would have to be one of the best tactical changes I've seen.

Who were your favourite defenders to play behind?

The back-four I had at Chelsea were unbelievable. We had Ron Harris, Dave Webb, John Dempsey and Eddie McCreadie, the 'four assassins' we called them. All four were strong, tough tacklers; the strongest and meanest back-four I played with.

Who was the best striker that ever played against you?

One of the best strikers of the ball I ever played against was Bobby Charlton. Not necessarily because of the power in his shooting, but because he was two-footed; he could hit the ball just as well with either foot, and you wouldn't know which side was his strongest. I saw it up-close from playing with England, he had tremendous poise and balance, he was one of the best.

Peter Lorimer at Leeds was another one, you were aware of these players' ability, and you had to be alert when they were on the ball. People who could hit the ball well would usually be looking to shoot from all over the place.

Who was the most aggressive striker you played against?

Without a doubt, Andy Lockhead. He was a Scottish international who played for Burnley, strong as an ox, and good in the air; on one occasion he knocked me out, not intentionally, but he was certainly the most physical fella I came up against.

Another one was Bobby Smith. When I first came on the scene in the '60s, Bobby played for Spurs; he was a tough centre-forward. Funnily enough, I saw him recently as well; I hadn't seen him for years, and I told him he used to like knocking me about, he said: "Yes, but in those days we were allowed to", and he was right.

Which current goalkeeper would you most compare yourself to?

They're all so big nowadays that it would be hard. I know Petr Cech at Chelsea, and when I look at him, I think to myself, if I was his height, I could have been a decent goalie. I can't compare myself to any because I'm so small.

How much do you think you'd be worth in today's market?

I haven't got a clue. The money's changed, it's unbelievable really, I wouldn't have a clue, and it's a difficult question because you can't equate it.

What do you make of the current generation of goalkeepers?

We have a lot of good goalkeepers, but we have a lot of foreign goalkeepers as well. If you look at the Premiership, there are only four or five goalies that play on a regular basis. Suffice to say, if you're not playing in the Premiership every week, you're not going to be international quality; you need to play to keep that consistency, so we have a problem.

I'm a big advocate of foreign players, and some of them have given our game a great service, but when it comes to goalkeepers, a lot of them are stopping home-grown talent being given a chance. We have the likes of Scott Carson and Ben Foster, who I rate highly, and Chris Kirkland, who's always getting injured. I was his coach at England Under-21 level, and he could be a good keeper if he didn't get injured so often. Joe Hart at Man City has great potential, but if they want somebody more experienced, he's not going to get the opportunity to improve.

These players would have had more of an opportunity in my day. It's like any business, the more experience you have from being at the top, the better you're going to be.

Would you have supported Carlo Cudicini making himself available for England?

Without a doubt. If he's good enough, and Carlo certainly is, here is another guy who's on the bench, and doesn't play regularly enough to prove himself, yet he's top-class. I think Chelsea have two of the best goalkeepers in the league, but only one can play. If you ask him though, I think you'd find that Carlo wants to play for Italy, and you can understand that.

With the average player these days being a multi-millionaire, do you feel that you were born at the wrong time?

Yes, I would be crazy if I said any different. I would like to have been born 30 years later, and then I could have had all that money, but I don't begrudge the players getting what they get. I enjoyed my time, and I wouldn't have changed it for the world, we were well paid at the time compared to the average wage, and I had a great life, we had good holiday's, decent cars etc, I'm thankful for that.

How would you have coped with the profile players have these days?

Well that's the thing I don't like about football nowadays. That's why I liked playing in my era, even though we didn't get the money. We were in the public eye, but people weren't watching us every minute of the day; we could go out to restaurants without being pestered, nowadays they can't breathe without something happening, so you can't lead a normal life.

They have a lot to put up with, and believe me, it's not easy. They are always in the spotlight, people like David Beckham can't just go shopping in the town centre, he has to have security, not just for himself, but for his family as well, and that must be awful. I'm sure a lot of players would love to lead a normal life, but unfortunately nowadays, once you get the fame and the money, you can't lead a normal life.

Who would you nominate as the best ever Chelsea player?

They've had so many it's hard. 'Ossie' stands out; he had so much ability and talent, a great character. Charlie Cooke also stands out; he could win games with his dribbling. Ron Harris in a different vein, tough man, he played so consistently, probably the best professional I ever played with, and one of the best man-markers in the game.

Of the more recent sides, the one who stands out is Zola. He's a lovely man, but his ability on the field was superb. They have had many great players, you could name loads, when they had their centenary a few years ago, they were picking the best players from the last 100 years, and it must have been so difficult.

You mentioned Peter Osgood, what's your favourite 'Ossie' memory?

There's so many, he was always winding you up 'Ossie'. We played a side from Luxembourg in the Fair's cup, and beat them 8-0 in the away leg. When we were getting ready for the home game, 'Ossie' told me he was going to score six, and in the end, we had a £5 bet.

We played the game, and 'Ossie' had scored five when we were awarded a penalty. John Hollins was due to take it, but 'Ossie' wanted to. He told everybody that I came running out of my goal and said that he couldn't take it. Anyway, John took it in the end and scored, I told 'Ossie' it served him right for being so big-headed, and saying he was going to score six.

What's your favourite Ron Harris memory?

We were playing against Sheffield Wednesday one week, and they were attacking down the left. Ron was playing right-back, and he caught the guy on the ball with a bad challenge. As the ball ran loose, another player controlled it, and Ron caught him as well, lastly, he took a third man out; he'd managed to injure three different players in the space of ten seconds, and they all had to receive treatment. It just shows what a strong character he was; he's a great fella, and I do a lot of work with him now. He's very funny, and anybody who's met him will know that.

Many fans still talk about the cup final replay in 1970.

Yes, it was very physical, as was the first game at Wembley. Leeds and Chelsea were great rivals in those days, they hated each other, and it was quite a battle. We were very lucky to get a draw at Wembley, the pitch was diabolical, and the ball didn't bounce, Leeds ran us ragged.

The replay was very physical, and our perseverance pulled us through. There were tackles flying in all over the place, and how nobody got seriously injured or sent off, I do not know to this day. There were incidents in that game constantly, because we were just two very competitive teams, luckily we came through in extra-time and won, so it was very memorable.

Do you remember picking up your injury?

Yes, I went up for a catch, and Mick Jones clattered me. He caught my knee with his own, and I must have hit a nerve. I couldn't go off as there was no substitute goalkeeper, so I had to get on with it. I have to credit my defenders because they did protect me a lot in that game.

That season, you were voted runner-up in the footballer of the year award. How did that feel?

I remember being voted the most entertaining player of the year by a magazine, but I don't remember the other award. I remember being presented with the magazine award by Bobby Moore, and I've still got the trophy. Getting awards was lovely, as it meant people appreciated what you did.

You mentioned winning the entertainment award. Was it something you were aware of?

No. You're not aware of things until they happen. The fact we got to the cup final meant that I stood out a lot more than some of the other players, so in that sense, I had an advantage.

What do you remember about the cup-winners-cup success in 1970-71?

I just remember that we got to another final so quickly. It was very pleasing to me because I'd been involved in the World Cup in Mexico, and received a bit of stick when we got beat by Germany. I was just pleased to get back on the winning track again. As a professional, you've got to accept criticism, but I wanted to prove people wrong. A lot of fans at away games had been giving me stick, so to get to a major final, and beat a great Real Madrid side, was more than pleasing, because of what had gone on previously, and the Chelsea fans were so supportive that year.

What were the funniest moments of your career?

We played Roma in the UEFA Cup one year. We beat them 4-1 in the home leg, and in the papers the next day, they were saying that we had called them animals. I'll never forget it, because Terry Venables scored a hat-trick, and Eddie McCreadie got sent off, but we still beat them 4-1.

The papers in Italy went mad, and that was one of the most hostile away games I played in. Even when the game had started, missiles were reining down on us. At one point, the Roma forward was through on goal, as I dived out to narrow the angle, a tomato which had been thrown from the crowd, obviously aimed at me, hit the Roma player straight in the face, and splashed all over their white kit.

On the field I was quite serious; I used to concentrate as much as I possibly could. 'Ossie' had a different attitude, even though he was a great professional, he used to humiliate opponents, with nutmegs and that sort of thing. As a goalkeeper though, you can't afford to take risks, because if you do, you concede a goal.

Who did you room with?

Bobby Tambling. We joined on the same day, and neither of us were from London; Bobby was from down near Portsmouth, and I was from Worthing. We were both fairly quiet, and we just hit it off, we roomed for years until he left for Crystal Palace in 1977. Bobby lives in Ireland now, but he still comes over for games, and it's always great to see him.

Were you a fan of training?

Yes, I was a fanatic. 'Ossie' and Marvin Hinton hated training, but I loved it, every day was a challenge, and where I was so small, I was a good runner, I used to win all the races. We used to do a cross-country run at Epsom, and I'd just been injured. Harry Medhurst, who was the physio, told me to take it easy and run at the back, so I was running along with 'Ossie' and 'Hutch', but 'Ossie' was more of a carthorse as he liked to put it, whereas I was a thoroughbred.

There was a famous trip to Blackpool, under Tommy Docherty, which many people say cost Chelsea the title.

Yes I remember it well. The next morning, Tommy came into our room and told us what had happened. Straight away, he sent the boys who were involved home, and I think that was a mistake. You have your drinkers in any club, but I wasn't really one for going to clubs after a game, I would prefer to have a drink in the hotel. The players who were sent home, originally thought it was just a joke, but when they got off the train at Kings Cross and saw the press, they realised how serious the situation was.

They had just gone out for a few drinks, but they'd broken the curfew, and one of the porters told Tommy. After they were sent home, we had four or five new players in the side and we lost 6-2. It messed our season up completely and it was a real shame. Tommy should have just taken the boys to one side and had a word, but he was a disciplinarian and that was it.

Terry Venables was reported to be an influential player at Chelsea. What was your relationship like with him?

Very good. You knew Terry was going to make a good coach. He got in the first-team just before me, and on the way back from games, he'd be making little notes on the opposition, he's so tactically aware, and has an unbelievable knowledge of the game.

He was a very good player as well, unfortunately, he fell out with Tommy Docherty because they had similar temperaments, they were both strong characters. Tommy wanted to be in charge, but Terry, who was our captain, was taking over the team talks, he was only speaking his mind, but Tommy didn't like it.

It was a shame to see Terry go. When I first met him, I used to really admire him, because he was such a confident guy, he was an extrovert, a leader, I used to look up to him a lot.

There was a game against Leeds, in 1967-68, when you had to pick the ball out of the net seven times. What do you remember about that?

I remember it very well. It was a time when we'd just lost our manager, it was coming towards the end of the season, and there were one or two players that weren't being professional. I remember ranting and raving at a few of the players, and one of them actually came up to me at the end of the game and apologised for his attitude. We were well and truly walloped that day.

Some people say your loyalty to Chelsea cost you a lot of money, in terms of signing-on fees. If you could turn back the clock, would you still show that same level of loyalty?

You are what you are, and I'm that sort of person, so yes, I probably would have. I enjoyed it so much there, and I was settled, I was happy at Chelsea, and didn't want to move just for money. In our day, being content and having the support of the fans was enough.

Were you aware of other clubs being interested in you?

Yes, West-Ham were interested in me at one point. It was around the time of the 1966 World Cup. There was talk about it, but nothing ever came of it. Tommy Docherty brought in Alex Stepney, because he knew I wanted to get away, having spent time with the West-Ham boys at the World Cup. He tried to play us off against each other, but it didn't work, as we were good mates. We told him that whoever he picked, it would be on merit.

The players had gone back to training while I was still away with England, and a few days before the World Cup final, the Chelsea secretary called, and said that Tommy wanted me to fly over to Germany and meet up with the rest of the team, immediately after the final. I told them I wanted a break, and Tommy wasn't happy, so after the final, I went away for a few days with my family; when I returned, Tommy reported it to the board, and they fined me a week's wages. Don't get me wrong, it's not a vendetta that's carried on. I still see Tommy now, and he's such a funny man, I think the world of him.

How did you feel when you heard Chelsea had signed Alex Stepney?

I was pleased, because I thought I was going to get away. I was driving home when I heard it on the news, and I almost crashed the car, I was pleased though. Our first game the next season was West-Ham away, and their boys were parading the World Cup.

It was Charlie Cooke's debut, and he scored in a 1-0 win. I also played a blinder, and Tommy kept me in the side. Three weeks later, he sold Alec Stepney; I was livid at the time, but obviously happy to stay at Chelsea in the end.

How did you hear about your first England call-up?

I honestly don't remember. I think in those days they wrote to you, it wasn't like nowadays, when the media get hold of it first. I had played in the Under-23 side regularly before I got the call-up, and I was playing well at Chelsea, so it wasn't a complete shock.

What was the mood like amongst the England squad of 1966?

Fantastic. The camaraderie was just like a club team, we all got on well together. Alf made sure that whatever we did, all 22 of us did it together; he kept reminding us that we were a team of 22, not 11. When I joined up, we went on a pre-World Cup tour, to Finland, Denmark, Norway and Poland. I made my debut in Denmark, and we won 2-0, but like any goalkeeper, I was really pleased to have kept a clean-sheet on my debut.

What memories stand out from that 1966 final?

We were all in the dressing-room before the game, and Alf asked those not involved, to leave the room. He said a steward would show us to our seats, but he added: "With five minutes to go, when we are winning, I want you all to come back down, so that we can celebrate together, you are as much a part of my team as the players on the pitch", and that's exactly what happened; as we approached the bench, with England leading 2-1, the Germans equalised.

We then spent the whole of extra-time, watching from the bench. I remember, as the team got further and further in the competition, having old women, who'd never watched the game before, wishing us luck, and it was a tremendous time, a big, big moment. We used to go everywhere together, we met the likes of Sean Connery and Cliff Richard, we were going to so many functions, just to get out of the hotel.

Was there a part of you that hoped Gordon Banks would get injured?

No, we were good mates, and still are. Every year, the whole '66 squad go away for a few days with our wives, and two people organise the trip. Well, next year, me and 'Banksy' are organising it, so we are in regular contact. He's a great man, and I was behind him all the way, and I'm sure he would have been the same if it was roles reversed.

Do you feel you should have won more England caps?

I would have loved to. I played seven times, and I must admit, the only game we lost was the 1970 World Cup quarter-final against Germany, which everybody remembers for my mistake. We won all the other six, and I only conceded one goal, so I regard my international career as a success. When you're playing with people like 'Banksy', you just have to accept it. I was back-up many times though.

Do you still follow Chelsea?

Without a doubt. I'm fortunate enough to do the match day hospitality, with Ron Harris and Kerry Dixon, and it's great. I love being part of Chelsea, I was involved with them for 29 years as a player and a coach, and it's nice to be back, they're in my blood.

How would Peter Bonetti like to be remembered?

For my contribution to football over forty years, as a player and a coach. Remember me for my goalkeeping career, and not just that one game in the 1970 World Cup, when I had a bad game, and to say I hope I helped people along the way with my coaching.

Bobby Tambling

Chelseas all-time record goal scorer and one of the nicest men in football

When did you first realise you was going to make a living from football?

I'll tell you a little story. At 13, we had a careers mistress come around the school, and she said: "What are you going to do when you leave school?", and I said I was going to be a pro' footballer. I looked at her and she just laughed. She said: "Yes, but what are you really going to do?", and I told her again, so she said:"Okay", and left it at that. Back in those days, I didn't know that I was going to make a career out of it, but that was the dream, and it's the same dream that thousands of lad's have had since, and will carry on having.

What inspired you to become a footballer?

I think it was all the books. In those days, we had no TV, it was the sports annuals that players wrote in, and when you're young you believe every story. I was a big fan of Blackpool, because of Stanley Mortensen, not Stanley Matthews. I remember when he scored in the cup final, and reading that he saw a gap in the wall, and drove the ball through it. I thought it was brilliant. Dreams are made from those sort of stories, and we had nothing visual to go by. It was those sort of stories that made you want to dream perhaps that one day you could play.

How did you learn about your trade?

I come from a large family. Five boys, and I was the youngest. They all played sport, and football was the most common. Being the youngest, I got to hear all the stories about the games. I can remember playing in a side when I was only 13, and I was playing against great big men. I was stuck out on the left-wing as it was the safest place for me, but as I was left-footed, it was the best place for me as I could play there. Those were experiences which helped me along.

Can you remember when you first heard of Chelsea's interest?

I played with the school team when I was ten, but I was playing with older lads. We got to go to the cup final, but I broke my arm and couldn't play. By the time I was 13, I'd been making progress towards the county side, and a scout (Mr Thompson) knocked on the door. That was the first time I knew professional clubs were looking at me.

Who else was interested at the time?

Wolves were interested when I was on the verge of leaving school. I was a fully-fledged schoolboy international by then, and there were a few clubs interested. If you remember the mid '50s, wolves were possibly the top club at the time, and I was very impressed that they were looking at me, and they were ready to sign me. I then played a bad game at Wembley for England schoolboys, and they said they weren't interested in signing me, then I played well against Northern Ireland, and they were back on the phone again, and that sort of behaviour doesn't impress even a 15 year-old bloke. So they were put to the back of the list. I met very interesting men at that stage. Harry Johnston, who was the Reading manager, wanted to sign me. He came and spoke to me, and he was a very nice guy. At the end of the evening, he said: "Can I just give you one bit of advice, if you're not going to join Reading, move away from your own area". He knew Portsmouth were interested in me, and basically told me not to go there, as I would have so many people that I knew, telling me what I was doing wrong every week. He told me to give myself a chance and move away, and it was good advice. I didn't move to Chelsea on that advice alone.

What was your first impression of Chelsea?

When I first went there, I was 15. I went for a tour, I had to meet Ted Drake, and I was in shock. I'd hardly ever been to a big stadium (unless I was playing), and I was in awe of Stamford Bridge. I don't remember meeting any players, but I remember meeting Ted, and having lunch with him. He was telling me how good Chelsea was for young players, and from that moment, I was going to be nothing but a blue.

What can you recall about your debut against West-Ham?

A really fantastic day for us. Barry Bridges and I were in digs together. We'd been that way ever since I'd come up to live in London, so we'd become good mates, and still are today. Ted Drake pulled us aside on the Thursday, and said there was a good chance that we'd both be making our debuts against West-Ham. Neither of us were that nervous initially, excited, but still normal. It wasn't until the team meeting before the game, that I started to realise I could be out of my depth. I started to get nervous then, I'm not sure if Barry was the same, but he was more confident and more experienced then me. I'd gone straight from the juniors into the first team. The older lads in the dressing room were very good, though the average age of our forward line that day was only 21, Peter Brabrook, Peter Cliss, 'Bridgo', Jimmy Greaves, and myself. The older players, like Peter Sillett, came up and just said: "Go out and do what you do in training", 'Bridgo' and myself both scored, and it was the stuff dreams are made of.

Chelsea were famous for having a great youth set up in the late '50s. What would you put that down to?

Jimmy Thompson. He could charm birds out of a tree, he was a real character, and you just loved him. Apart from him, he was the leader; they must have had a brilliant scouting system, because they were the best in the south for getting youngsters. People forget though, whilst they had brilliant youngsters, the people at the helm had the confidence to play these lads, and that's why I signed for Chelsea. Not only did they have a brilliant system, but they used that system to bring players through.

You mentioned you were in digs with Barry Bridges, who did you room with at Chelsea in your senior days?

Another pure gentleman, Peter Bonetti. We were in the youth team together, and we grew to be very close, sharing a room for eight or nine years, he's a great mate.

Obviously people remember Peter for being a great keeper, but what's he like off the pitch?

As I said, he's a pure gentleman. He would do anything for you; he's funny, without being over the top. He's somebody that you could rely on, and that you could call a mate.

Early in your career, despite playing really well, Chelsea were relegated. How did you feel, given that on a personal level, you'd had a good season, scoring 24 goals?

There was a bit of upheaval. Tommy Docherty had taken over, and wanted to implement his own ideas, but the senior players didn't like that. It was mainly down to the lack of experience. We had a lot of talented players, as the next season would show, but we were made to play for our inexperience.

Having had a taste of top-flight football, and being relegated, how tempted were you to look for a transfer in order to move up to Division 1?

It never occurred to me, it wasn't like today, where transfer rumours appear constantly, there wasn't so much of it back then. No, it never crossed my mind to leave Chelsea. I enjoyed myself there, and thought the future looked bright.

You touched on Tommy Docherty earlier on. What were your first impressions of him, and how did you feel about him giving you the captaincy?

He first joined the club as a player-coach. As a player, he was a joker who had to be the centre of attention in the dressing room. He was a very funny guy, and to suddenly be calling him 'boss' was a bit difficult, especially for the older players. Tommy was full of enthusiasm, and a guy that you either loved or hated, but however you felt about him, he could get you to play.

Some liked him, and would have run through a brick wall for him, those who didn't like him, would get so wound up by him, that they wanted to show him they were good enough to be in the side. Dave Sexton was a brilliant coach, and he loved continental football, he brought a lot of good ideas into the club.

As a former captain yourself, what qualities do you think make a good captain?

The rest of the lad's respect you, either through the way you are on and off the field, whether you demand respect, or whether people give you respect because of your own conduct. You have got to be able to listen to people and see their problems, and be able to sort out little hiccups that might occur between players and coaching staff.

The following season, in Chelsea's promotion winning season, you scored an incredible 35 goals, which was half the teams total. As a young kid, how much pressure did you feel to score goals?

No pressure at all. We were playing exciting football, we were all young and fit, passing the ball with pace, and in Terry Venables, we had the best passer of the ball of that time. What stood out for me with Terry, was that he wouldn't make the obvious pass; he would pick a pass that only class players could make. When you made a run you knew if anybody could pick you out, it was him, and we were always willing runners.

Were you aware from playing with Terry, that he had the potential to forge a successful management career?

Yes, because he was always talking football. We would go to the café when we were in the youth team, and there were always points to discuss, he was always a deep-thinker who was prepared to do something different.

One of your career highlights must be the league cup victory, what do you remember about that day?

It was slightly disappointing in the sense that in those days, it was played over two legs, so we actually won a cup final with a dull 0-0 draw in Leicester. We'd had an exciting game at Stamford Bridge which we won 3-2, and it'll always be remembered for the goal that Eddie McCreadie scored. He ran from the inside his own half to score, and that will always stick in Chelsea fans minds.

Having won the League Cup, does it sadden you these days to see so many clubs downgrade it?

Yes, and even the FA Cup. In the early rounds, sides are fielding all of their youngsters, which is great for those players, but I think it lessens the impact of the cup. The cup has always been a tremendous draw for players and fans alike, and to play in a cup final was one of the highlights of a player's career.

There are a number of legends who actually never got to play in a cup final, and now you see clubs that can't be bothered until they get to the latter stages. Yes, it upsets me that the game has turned that way. To finish fourth in the league, is now seen as more of an achievement then winning the cup final.

You scored a consolation goal in the '67 cup final defeat against Tottenham. What do you remember about that day?

In the '60s we were always a good cup side. In the two years previous, we'd been losing semi-finalists, so we thought it would be third time lucky when we beat Leeds in the semi-final. To play against Spurs, who now had Terry Venables in their side, was very exciting, but it was dampened in the build-up to the game, due to a ticket dispute between the club and the players. That slightly took our minds off the ball, and then to make sure nobody got injured, we took it fairly easy in the run up to the game. Old professionals will tell you, you can't turn your form on and off like a tap, and by the time we stepped out at Wembley, nine of us absolutely froze, we never competed. Even when we scored the goal with eight or nine minutes left, we still didn't worry them. It was very disappointing for the players and fans.

Can you still remember your goal now?

I like other people to remember it. They say : "You scored a header at Wembley", and I say : "Yes", and leave it at that, because to be honest, I went up for a cross with Pat Jennings, it looked like he was going to get there, but to my amazement, he missed it, and it hit me on the head and went in. It looked a lot better on the news then from where I saw it. It's a nice one for the memory.

Another game fondly remembered by Chelsea fans, is the 6-2 win at Villa Park, when you scored an amazing five goals.

Yes, that was a fantastic team really. We had 'Ossie' (Peter Osgood), George Graham, Johnny Hollins, there was so much talent there, and Villa were going strongly at that time. We were both in the top three, and it was one of those days when everything clicked as a team. Goals came from everywhere, I have to remind people of this, but three of the goals came with the 'wooden' right leg. Then after about 70 Minutes, I'd signalled to come off as I had a twinge in my knee, and as I signalled, Johnny Boyle made a jog through the middle and I thought I'd see what happens, Johnny ended up dragging everybody towards him, so when he pulled it back to me, I had a simple tap-in.

Did that make your knee feel a bit better?

Well, I often wondered whether I could have stayed on and gone for the record, which was seven, but to be honest, it never crossed my mind.

What do you recall about your first England call-up?

A bit of fun really. The day it came, I was on the treatment table at Stamford Bridge. I wasn't badly injured, but fancied an early day. Tommy Docherty came down and asked how bad the injury was. I told him I'd be okay for Saturday. He then told me I'd better be ready for tomorrow, because I had to go and play for England against Wales, and I tell you what, you've never seen someone move so fast, I was very proud to play for my country.

You mention you were capped three times for England. Some people say you should have been capped a lot more.

Well, I look at the players that were around at the time. Jimmy Greaves was a Rolls-Royce of a goalscorer. I played with him at Chelsea, and he was brilliant to play with. He knew where the goal was instinctively, he was like silk. People say I took over from him, which I did, but we were as different as chalk and cheese, and so I couldn't see myself keeping him out of the England side at all. It's nice of people to say I should have won more caps, but you have to remember the quality of the players I was competing with.

What was it like playing in an era when England were world champions?

I think that was probably the pinnacle of English football. It was great to just be in and around the international side, it was something to be proud of, and that's how we all felt. They talk about the Premiership now, and it probably is one of the best league's in the world, but in the '60s and '70s, English football was at its best.

Would you have swapped your three England caps for an illustrious career with Scotland or Ireland, had you been eligible?

No, I'm proud to be English. I won caps for England from being a schoolboy, through to the first-team, so no; I wouldn't want to play for anybody else.

What was your most memorable game in a Chelsea shirt?

There were some big games. On a personal level, the 6-2 win against Aston-Villa, because I scored five goals, and I didn't do that every week. As a young team, the win at Liverpool, when we beat them 2-1 in the cup. We went to Liverpool and played them off the pitch, and even to this day, not many teams do that, we gave them a goal start, and then played them off the pitch, winning 2-1. I don't think they had any complaints that day.

How would you describe the feeling of scoring a goal?

Well, for some players, scoring goals is everything, and that's how it was with me. To see the ball in the back of the net, even if it was the crappiest goal, was fantastic, if it was a super goal, that only made the feeling even better. The way we all celebrated in those days, it was as if we'd all scored, it was a real team effort. To realise now, the excitement the fans feel, is wonderful, you realise the excitement you're giving people.

Kerry Dixon was only nine goals away from beating your record at Chelsea. How were you feeling when he got closer?

My partner Val and I were living in Portsmouth. Every week I used to coach a side, and I'd rush home to get the results, and find out who had scored the goals. I remember a guy ringing me up, and at this stage I'd never met Kerry, if I had met him, I'd probably have been on the phone after every game, because he is one hell of a nice guy. The man on the phone asked me how I'd feel, once Kerry took my record. I told him I'd be disappointed, because it took me a lifetime to achieve, and to see that achievement no longer mean anything, I'd be disappointed , then all of a sudden, Kerry's not at Chelsea, and the record's safe for a little while longer.

There is a rumour that he's thinking of getting his boots back on.

I might have to pay him a visit. Ha ha

Do you think your record's safe forever given the lack of loyalty in the game?

No. I think Chelsea being the club they are now, they will find a super young striker, and they are a big enough club to keep super, young players, for any length of time, so there will be someone out there with the same hunger Kerry and I had, and hopefully they'll come along and join Chelsea

What was your relationship like with the Chelsea fans?

I loved them, I always had the feeling they liked me. People would often ask me if I'd heard comments. I always had the feeling the crowd was behind me, and I would love to play at Chelsea's ground now. The way the ground is now, is how we dreamt it would one day be. We always wanted the ground to be closed in, so we could get the marvellous atmosphere even bigger and better.

Which modern-day footballer would you most compare yourself to?

I was an out-and-out goalscorer, a fox in the box, and to me that's like Michael Owen. Michael Owen does his best work in the last third of the field. 'Bridgo' and I were both quick, so we played a style of football where we caught sides on the break. I then played with 'Ossie' and George Graham, who were great at finding you in the box. Charlie Cooke would supply you from one wing, and Peter Houseman did the same from the other. Ian Hutchinson was so brave. He'd knock down three defenders for you to run through, and playing with these players was fantastic, they made scoring goals easy.

How much do you think you would be worth in today's transfer market?

Players who score goals are always expensive. If I could score the same amount of goals today, as I did in my day, I'd be very expensive. Each player has a time when he plays. My style suited the era I played in. Whether that would be the same today, I don't know. People say: "Can you teach somebody to score goals?" I don't think you can. Nobody taught Jimmy Greaves, it was his own instinct, mine was the same. You practice shooting so that you can shoot accurately, but to be in the position to score goals, that comes with instinct.

On the theme of money. We live in an era where very average players are multi-millionaire's. Do you ever look back and wish you were born 30-40 years later?

People would call me a fool if I said money doesn't bother me, and I wouldn't enjoy earning that much, of course I would. But the nature of the game has changed, I don't know if I could handle the way the game is nowadays. They are built up to be superstars, and everybody knows them. We were just normal guys living our dreams, but we could still go and have a beer in a local pub, without being bothered all night, that can't happen today. Everything has a price; the price of being famous today, is that you lose your privacy.

How would you have coped with the fame, having paparazzi following you around etc?

I don't know. I'm very shy, and I don't know if I could've handled that. People like David Beckham...... to me, he handles it brilliantly. There are many others as well. It doesn't matter how big a player you are, or how small the town, it's going to be the same everywhere. It must be very difficult for the lads to handle.

In your final season at Chelsea, you were unlucky with injuries, coupled with the fact there was a Peter Osgood coming into the side. How do you recall that period?

Peter had been in the side for a few years now, and we'd played together quite successfully. When certain things happen, people change, and their role in the side changes. I picked up an injury early in the season, and from that point onwards, I didn't stay fit for any long period. I was out for three months, and loaned out to Crystal Palace to regain fitness, and got injured again as soon as I was back. There were two of us, Alan Birchall and myself, who had been out injured all season, and the side had settled down. Dave had made a very successful side, and he wasn't going to change that for anybody. Peter Houseman was having a brilliant season on the left, providing the ammunition for 'Hutch' and 'Ossie'. The lad that benefited the most from our absences was Alan Hudson. Things like that happen in football, it's full of ups and downs. I'd had lucky breaks in my career, and that was a lucky break for Alan, which he took. The last goal I scored for Chelsea was before I was 28, and I thought I was old. I was heartbroken that I had to leave Chelsea. I hoped Dave would try and talk me into staying, but he didn't, so I moved on.

How hard was it to leave Chelsea for Crystal Palace?

Heartbreaking, because I loved the FA Cup, and that's proven by my record in the competition. We'd been so close, losing in the final, two semi-finals, and numerous quarter finals, and then the year I couldn't make the team, Chelsea go and win it. Now don't get me wrong it was fantastic for the lads, but more so, for the fans, because the fans can't do anything about it. When you're a player, you can actually rectify things, but when you're a fan you're just sitting there hoping. For me though, seeing the lads win the cup without me, just made me think that maybe I should move on. I remember speaking to Eddie McCreadie shortly after I'd moved, and he said he wished he'd spoken to me before I left, because he felt if I got my fitness back.........and he was right, I should of hung in there. Dave had brought new players in, and what can you say.

How do you reflect back on the Palace years?

Lovely club, really nice guys there. It was a good experience to go somewhere different, and see the game from a different aspect. I worked with different people at Palace. George Petchey was a wonderful coach; he was very much like Dave, a nice guy. But the club weren't set up to be where they were, which was in the top league. The time I was there, reflected that, because it was always a struggle. They were desperate to stay in the big-time. It was hard for me to follow being with a great club, being with a good club.

In 1973 you moved to Ireland, playing for Cork-Celtic, helping them win the LOI title, how did that come about?

Through an old mate of mine, Paddy Mulligan, I'd had achilles trouble at Palace, which almost finished my career. The doctor told me that the only way to help my injury was to play on wet grass. Paddy told me the surface in Ireland was permanently wet and soft, so he fixed me up with a club. He told me they were the best club in Cork, which wasn't true. For the first year I was still living in England, travelling back and forth. My mates at Palace gave me a lot of stick for the move, but at the end of the season, I took great pleasure in telling them we were in Europe.

Is it true that when you were about to sign on the dotted line, you received a call telling you to check the surface before signing?

Very true. I'd flown, into Cork to sign, and I received a call from Dave McCuzzy, who was the manager of another Cork side. He told me not to sign anything. He said anything Celtic were offering, his club (Cork-Hibs) would better. He said everything about his club was better, but I told him I had given them my word, and I was going to sign. He asked me to promise him one thing. He said if he couldn't change my mind before I signed, ask them to show me the pitch, because he thought after seeing that pitch I wouldn't want to sign for them. When I went back to the Cork-Celtic officials and told them who the call had been from, they went into a state of panic. I insisted they showed me the pitch, but they wanted me to sign first. Eventually, they ran me down to the ground, and it was no Wembley, but I'd played on many similar pitches, and I'd given them my word, so I signed, and we won the league, so it was happy days all around.

I was at my first training session. The Cork lads had strong accents, and I sat in between two of them. When they spoke to each other, I didn't have a clue what they were talking about. All of a sudden, there was a flurry of movement underneath the seat, I turned to one of the lads and asked if he'd seen what I had, a big rat. He told me it was the team's cat, and they all fell about laughing. They took me on a tour of the dressing-room, which consisted of three showers, for both teams to share. It was back to basics, but brilliant. It doesn't matter what level you play at, if you have a good dressing-room, which is a laugh, but serious when it matters, that instils team-spirit in a side. I look at Chelsea now, and the team spirit within Chelsea is absolutely fantastic. They are so mentally strong. They don't always go out there and play the best football, but they don't ever look like they're going to get beat. I think that comes room the dressing-room strength they have.

You stayed on in Ireland, and tried your hand at management, how was that?

It was fairly up and down. I've only managed a couple of pro' clubs. Football in those days was very skimpy, they only worked from session to session. The real success came from the local clubs, boys who worked all week, came to training shattered from work, and give you two hours effort in the pouring rain, it was fantastic. I only did it because I couldn't get football out of my system. If you can give somebody a chance to enjoy the things you've enjoyed, then you're doing some good. I'm still coaching lads of 18, and when I see lads I used to coach, who are now 24-25, they give me so much respect, and it makes me proud, they almost treat me like their dad, and it makes you feel good. It's fantastic to give that pleasure to people, especially as football has given me so much.

Who's the best player you ever played against?

To me, Georgie Best had everything. He was only slight up-close, and throughout his career he had some of the biggest men kicking lumps out of him. He still got up and produced the goods. 'Greavsie' was fantastic. He was so cool, so funny, and sometimes slightly nervous, but on the pitch he was deadly.

In terms of players you played with, what's your favourite memory of 'Chopper'?

Missing me with a tackle in training I would think. We were in Venezuela, playing in a three team tournament. When the other two sides played against each other, we sat in the stands watching, Porto had a winger that was lightning, and somebody asked Ron how he was going to deal with him, and Ron replied : "He can't run that fast with no legs". When we played Porto, the winger had showed Ron the ball a couple of times and whizzed past him. Somebody told Ron to stop him before he caused us any major problems, but Ron couldn't get a tackle in. Eventually the ball came to Ron, and it looked as though he'd failed to control it, but he'd purposely let the ball run away from him, so the winger had to get it. Ron gave him such a clatter that we never saw the winger again, and that summed Ron up for me. He was a hard lad, but shrewder than people gave him credit for. Ron was a very good player though, there was more to him then just clobbering people, and the fact that he played so many games for Chelsea, and led them to so much success proves that.

You also played with Peter Osgood. What's your favourite 'Ossie' memory?

He had so much skill, but he was a timid lad when he first came into the side which may surprise people. After he came back from a broken leg, he reacted brilliantly. He could play as a midfielder because he could play balls through the eye of a needle. He had such good control. The only thing he lacked was genuine pace, but he had so much else which more than made up for that.

Did you have a nickname?

'Bridgo' liked to call me 'Jumbo' because of my ears, and that stuck the whole time I was at Chelsea. Even now when we meet up people still use it.

What are you up to these days Bobby?

I'm still involved in football. I do the under -18's in the village I live in, which I love, and the boys are great fun to be around.

How would Bobby Tambling like to be remembered?

For enjoying his football, and enjoying Chelsea.

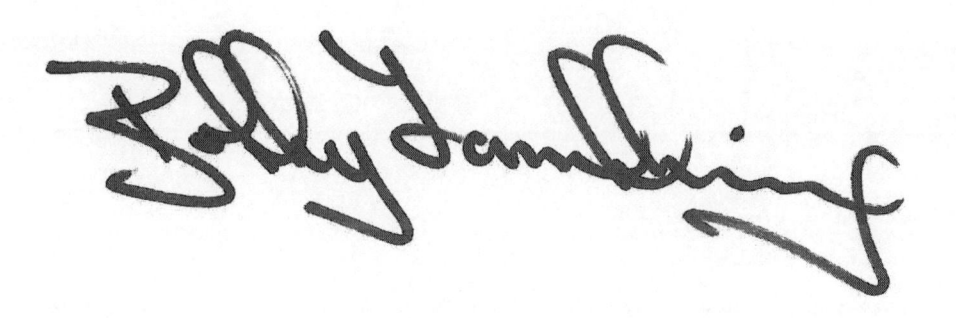

You can get fully signed limited edition audio versions of each interview

Every collectors set comes complete with a certificate of authenticity signed by the legend and individually numbered set

Plus a unique signing session photo

For more information and hundreds of other pieces of Chelsea memorabilia

Check out the official 60 minutes with ... website

www.60mins.tv

For more information on how to book

Ron "Chopper" harris
Peter Bonetti
Bobby Tambling
Kerry Dixon

For media, after dinner , corporate or private signing sessions

Please contact the 60 minutes with... agency on

0845 003 7465

email shop@60mins.tv

Printed in Great Britain
by Amazon.co.uk, Ltd.,
Marston Gate.